On With the Story

Adolescents Learning Through Narrative

Susan Y. Wanner

Boynton/Cook Publishers
HEINEMANN
Portsmouth, NH

Boynton/Cook Publishers, Inc.
A subsidiary of Reed Elsevier Inc.
361 Hanover Street, Portsmouth, NH 03801-3912
Offices and agents throughout the world

Editor: Peter Stillman
Production: Nancy Sheridan
Cover design: Darci Mehall
Front cover photo: © Elaine Rebman

The author and publisher wish to thank the following for permission to
reprint copyrighted material in this book:

Page 38: Excerpt from "I always called her Aunt Susie" copyright © 1981
by Leslie Marmon Silko. Reprinted from *Storyteller* by Leslie Marmon
Silko, published by Seaver Books, New York, New York.

Page 130: Excerpt reprinted by permission of the publishers from NAR-
RATIVE FROM THE CRIB edited by Katherine Nelson, Cambridge,
Mass.: Harvard University Press, copyright © 1989 by the President and
Fellows of Harvard College.

Every effort has been made to contact the copyright holders and students
for permission to reprint borrowed material. We regret any oversights
that may have occurred and would be happy to rectify them in
future printings of this work.

Library of Congress Cataloging-in-Publication Data

Wanner, Susan Y.
    On with the story : adolescents learning through narrative / Susan
Y. Wanner.
        p.   cm.
    Includes index.
    ISBN 0-86709-337-4
    1. Narration (Rhetoric) — Study and teaching.   I. Title.
LB1631.W24 1994
808'.042'0712 — dc20   94-5587
                                                            CIP

Printed in the United States of America on acid-free paper
98 97 96 95 94 CC 1 2 3 4 5 6 7 8 9

To my mentors:
Michael Armstrong
Tony Burgess
Jim Reid

Contents

Acknowledgments

My career as a student has spanned five decades, during which I have been on the receiving end of some superb teaching. I would like to thank these people, each of whom has opened up windows into the magic of learning:

My mother, Elinor Yocom, taught me to love language, and taught me a lot of language to love.

My father, Kenneth Yocom, was a great storyteller; he made distant and long-dead relatives as real to me as the parents and brothers I saw every day.

Margaret Hay taught senior English at Lower Merion High School. Her class was a fine mix of discovery and discipline.

Wayne Booth was writing his ground-breaking book, *The Rhetoric of Fiction*, when I was a freshman in his Masterworks class at Earlham College. He led that class through an exhilarating, dizzying year on the cutting edge of critical thought.

John and Marjorie Hunt, teacher/friends from Earlham days to the present, have given me generous, constant affirmation.

Warren Staebler at Earlham and Alan (Mokler) MacVey of the Middlebury College Bread Loaf School of English taught me how to love and teach Shakespeare.

I am indebted to all my professors at Bread Loaf. This book is a direct outgrowth of my study there. I am especially grateful to the program director, James Maddox, who has gone out of his way to be helpful, and to writing teachers James Britton, Ken Macrorie, and David Huddle.

Bread Loaf professors Michael Armstrong and Tony Burgess showed me the path, provided the push to bring this book into existence, and repeatedly brought me back on track during the writing process. To both, my deepest thanks.

I wish also to acknowledge these people who have made me a better teacher:

Jim Reid taught me how to teach *kids*.

The school board of Mt. Abraham Union High School has encouraged and generously supported my professional growth.

Mt. Abe administrators and teachers have been unstintingly supportive. I'm especially indebted to Tom Tailer and Chris Morgan for sharing their stories; to Melanie Stultz-Backus and Rich Steggerda for talking through some sticky ideas with me; to Karl Thelen for his help with the chapter on storytelling; and to David Marshak and Melissa Malcolm for sharing valuable resources.

Thanks also to the ninth-grade interdisciplinary teachers, Larry Brewer, Reva Cousino, Mark Johnson, Carol Kress, June Sargent, Margaret Snelgrove, Shelley Snyder, and Michele Wendel, from whom and with whom I have learned so much.

To my wonderful students—those whose work appears here and all the others—you're what it's all about. Thank you!

Four people provided outstanding support during the long and often lonely writing process:

Editor Peter Stillman treated me with good humor, high expectations, and patience, patience, patience.

My son Mark Wanner, also an editor, always knew what I should do and how to do it.

As the book took shape, Barry Lane contributed insight, encouragement, constructive criticism, and the practical advice of one who's been there before. The whole project has been more professional and better directed because of his involvement.

Most important of all has been the support of my husband, Jim Wanner. He sacrificed financial savings and wifely companionship; sent me off to the Bread Loaf Lincoln College campus at Oxford for seven weeks to start the actual writing; kept my computer tools up to date and working perfectly; talked me through confusion, discouragement, and cognitive swamps; read the early drafts and told me I had worthwhile things to say. Ultimately it was his faith in the project that made it happen.

≡*One*

Narrative as a Learning Medium in Adolescence and Beyond

*A*ll teachers worthy of the name are storytellers. It is through stories that we are best able to share with learners the vitality and relevance of our knowledge. Walk through the corridors of any high school, eavesdrop at the classroom doors: everywhere teachers are bringing their discipline alive by telling stories to illustrate, clarify, exemplify.

Tom Tailer's physics class, for example, has begun its study of electricity by building a bridge of crystal diodes. Tom equates the behavior of electrons to that of the Billy Goats Gruff:

"The goats want to cross the bridge because they see this pasture on the other side. What motivates them?"

A student suggests, "Hunger."

"Hunger, yes. And what motivates the electrons? Electromotive force, EMF. EMF is the electrons' equivalent of hunger.

"So, there's a bridge. The billy goats want to go across, but there's this troll that stops them. The first little goat goes across, trip, trop, trip, trop. He escapes the troll by saying, 'Look, there's a larger hunger coming behind me.' But he can't go back the other way across the bridge, because the troll will get him. Diodes let electrons pass in one direction but not in the other.

"The second billy goat gets across the same way, but the hunger of the third is too great. Send over too large a billy goat, or too large an electric force, and you destroy not only the troll but also the bridge."

Tom, a science teacher deeply interested in the symbolic nature of language, is careful to point out to his students that the

1

story of the Billy Goats Gruff is a metaphor, not scientific truth. "Science teachers use hosts of metaphors and stories that approximate the observable phenomena and then tell kids this is the truth—but it's not, even though it helps them understand. There are different ways of knowing. Any theory is just the latest version of the story of science."

Not all stories told in the classroom deal with academics. Sometimes teachers tell personal stories to model a particular behavior or to establish rapport with a class. Chris Morgan, consulting teacher, has been listening to a group of her special-ed students grumbling about their dislike and fear of tests.

"Well," she tells them, "you have to understand, I *really don't like snakes*. I just don't have much stomach for them. And once I had this bouncy kid—I liked him so much; but John, he always had things going on. It was the end of the year, exam time, but he wasn't so much worried about exams as he was about getting his locker cleaned out.

"So upstairs we went to his locker and he whipped out a great big garbage bag. Well, you've never seen a locker so full of *stuff*. It was like a coat that a magician has, the kind that stuff keeps coming out of. I noticed on the shelf he had this jar with things floating around in it. So I asked him, 'What's that?'

"He kind of shoved it in my face, and he said, 'Well, these are snake heads. I like to chop the heads off snakes and keep them.' And there were about a dozen snake heads floating around in alcohol.

"I couldn't believe it! But I was cool; I said, 'Oh! Okay, just keep them out of my sight!' So he put them in the bottom of the bag. And we kept pulling stuff out of the locker until he had this gigantic green garbage bag, like Santa's pack.

"He carried it downstairs, and all of a sudden at the bottom of the stairs he said, 'Ugh! This is heavy!' He just dropped it on the floor in front of me. Well, the jar of snake heads was in the bottom of the bag. The bag split open, the jar broke, and there I was standing in this puddle of alcohol and snake heads. I really thought I was going to lose it."

The students laugh, as Chris intended.

"I think it's a funny story, a joke on me. It forms a bond. I point out to them that there are things we don't like, or avoid, or both, and we find ourselves standing in the middle of them. We laugh at ourselves and our own fears."

Another important function of stories is to build community in the classroom. In English class, at my request, Jared reads aloud his narrative poem, "The Beast," about his aunt's death from cancer. It ends:

> ... the beast kept growing
> All over her body
> And she suffered terribly.
> Near the end,
> She couldn't eat
> Nor talk
> Nor see
> Nor walk
> Nor be touched
> When she needed to be held the most.
> She just lay in her bed
> In agonizing pain
> Waiting for the beast to win.
>
> The beast won
> On a cold Monday morning
> In the small hours of dawn
> But my Aunt Johnie is all right now
> Safe in the sky;
> And the cancer is dead
> Buried in the ground.
>
> —*Jared, 18*

Jared's classmates sit forward in their seats, intent, involved. When he has finished, they begin to talk, connecting his narrative with stories of their own memories and the ideas they evoke: "I remember when my grandfather died ... " "It's so hard when you want to help and there's nothing you can do ..." "I like what you said at the end; when somebody dies you really want them to be free ... "

The shared experience of Aunt Johnie's death, calling forth echoes of family deaths with which they have grappled on their own, brings these students together in knowledge and sympathy. On such shared experiences are cultures built and sustained. In any classroom, the stories in which everyone participates form a web that helps bind a diverse group into a functioning unit.

Developmental Theory and the Loss of Narrative

Intuitively, almost all teachers understand the educational power of stories. Teachers of adolescents weave anecdotes and parables into their classroom practice, and it's a good thing they do; because otherwise narrative virtually disappears from the high school and college curriculum. The instinct that prompts teachers to tell stories runs hard into educational theory that demands analytical and argumentative thinking from everyone past the age of thirteen. As a general rule, teachers may tell stories, but their teenage or young adult students may not. Jared's opportunity to share his own narrative is the exception, even in English class, where "story" has become "Literature": material written by a stranger from another time and place, and presented, not as an event to be incorporated into one's life experience, but as an icon to be revered and analyzed.

It's a crime to separate teenage and young adult learners from their stories. We do it in part, ironically, because Piaget says we can (not that we *should*; that we *can*). Piaget, who first identified developmental stages in learning, showed that true concept formation is not developmentally possible until adolescence. This is *not* to say that earlier modes of learning are inferior, nor that they should be abandoned after puberty. In some disciplines, symbolic conceptual learning builds upon the more concrete earlier modes: math, for example, incorporates arithmetic into algebra and other more abstract forms. However, when it comes to language, far too many American educators simply drop narrative in favor of what James Britton terms *transactional writing*—the more cognitively advanced rhetorical forms of exposition, argument, and analysis—as soon as children are deemed "ready."

Lev Vygotsky, a contemporary of Piaget's, has received a great deal of attention in the last twenty years because of his work demonstrating the interdependency between language and learning. Unlike Piaget, he does not see cognitive development as a simple function of growing older, but more as a dynamic interrelationship of maturity and learning—a combination, as it were, of nature and nurture. He describes adolescence in terms with which any high school teacher must agree as "less a period of completion than one of crisis and transition" and warns that

> it would be erroneous . . . to imagine that this transition from [cognitive] complexes to concepts is a mechanical process in which the higher developmental state completely supersedes the lower one. The developmental scene turns out to be much more complex. . . . We know fairly well that human actions do not belong necessarily to the highest and the most advanced level of development. Developmentally late forms coexist in behavior with younger formations. (1986, 140)

Much of Vygotsky's work is devoted to demonstrating the vital importance of narrative to early learning. Children are already steeped in story by the time they enter school. From infancy they hear the stories that orient them within their family and their culture. As soon as they acquire language, children begin to spin stories of their own, structuring their play with a running narrative that helps them make sense of the world and locate themselves as individuals in their social setting. This sort of play defines rules for behavior (Vygotsky 1978, 96) and permits children to explore safely, in fantasy, a range of possible realities. Transferring their fears to the wicked witch and the domestic details of their life and culture to their toys, they live and learn by metaphor, as the term is defined by Coleridge: "Imagination in action" (Mair 1976).

Because storytelling is always tied to the concrete, a representation of a particular event occurring in a particular place to particular characters, it precedes abstract thinking as a human cognitive skill. But just because metaphoric concept formation occurs developmentally *prior* to rational concept formation does not mean that it is *inferior* to it. At the highest levels, these two conceptual paths converge: metaphor and hypothesis are two sides of the same coin; both propose new connections that expand our knowledge of the world. For many adolescents, trying to make that conceptual shift from the concrete to the abstract, narrative as a means of shaping the world provides a useful bridge—"an intermediate level of generalization" (Burgess 1990). But there is a troll under that bridge, too, preventing access; regrettably, the troll is often the teacher.

Disciplinary Discourse and the Loss of Narrative

By and large, teachers in elementary school use narrative effectively. They encourage their pupils to read, write, and tell stories in part because they know that narrative is a sound learning medium for preadolescent children. Of course they teach formal elements: spelling, basic grammar, factual questions—the stuff of workbooks. But most teachers of young children realize also that in their job the most important things to teach are skills and behaviors; subject matter is secondary. Grade school teachers deal unambiguously with *children*. They tend to encourage all aspects of narrative because they are aware that children will learn and grow as much from reading stories, and from sharing their own and each other's stories, as from studying a textbook.

But increasingly in middle school through high school and college, the sense of just what a teacher is and ought to be teaching becomes confused. There's a world of difference between saying "I teach third grade" (a group of children), "I teach English" (a discipline), and "I teach Shakespeare" (a specialty). The more teachers perceive themselves to be teaching a *subject* rather than *people*, the more they are likely to shift their emphasis from the discoveries of learners to the discourse of a particular discipline. Rather than seeing students as individuals grappling with ideas, they see them as neophytes who must be trained to fit particular information into a specific scholarly linguistic mold.

Teachers of adolescents—college trained, steeped in the language forms of their own discipline, and driven by the school's demand for assessment—tend to confuse style with substance. They expect students unfamiliar with both the content and the form of discourse pertinent to their subject to master content and form together. For example, a chemistry student is supposed to be able to formulate the results of his experiment into a proper lab report, or a student of English literature might be required to respond to a great book with a literary analysis paper. But that isn't the way learning works. A great deal of messy rearrangement has to go on in a learner's head in order to accommodate a newly introduced concept and make it his own.

The sad fact is that students who succeed in achieving formal correctness tend prematurely to cut off their own conceptual exploration and development. This is true because the language of the learner just grasping an idea is different from the language of the expert communicating knowledge. Adolescents (and indeed most adults) who are trying to assimilate new information need to deal with it convergently, to integrate it into a wider spectrum of experience, including the senses and the emotions. These personal responses characteristically find voice first in informal, expressive writing or in narrative. Students who try to fit them into the divergent, abstract language required by disciplinary discourse may produce odd hybrid genres. Typically, teachers find the form lacking and overlook the real learning that has taken place. Thus teachers become formal critics rather than a supportive audience to their students. But, as Lil Brannon says,

> developing writers need to write often to trusted readers, people who are more interested in what the writers have to say than in the formal and technical lapses that the discourse might manifest ... writing abilities develop when people are afforded opportunities to exercise their natural human competence to make and share meaning by writing in a variety of modes for their own purposes to many different audiences. (1985, 19)

7

When the Schools Council Research group in England produced its ground-breaking study, *The Development of Writing
Abilities (11-18)* (Britton et al. 1975), the authors found that they
were unable even to use the common rhetorical terms (*analysis,
exposition*, etc.) to classify or evaluate student writing. Adolescents simply don't write in pure genres. The authors express
concern that the requirements of curriculum and assessment
limit students' writing options, and hence their development as
writers; and they urge teachers to be more receptive to speculative, expressive, and "poetic" (including narrative) writing from
adolescents.

The Loss of Personal and Oral Narrative

It is a mistaken notion too common in American high schools that
narrative has already served its purpose as a medium for learning
by the time a student enters ninth grade. Typically, high school
students have little opportunity to tell stories except in an elective
"creative writing" class, where the emphasis may be primarily on
form, or in a journal that is often overvalued (i.e., graded) or
undervalued (i.e., not read) by the teacher. Yet narrative is the one
rhetorical form in which teenagers are already competent. Just at
the age when they might bring rational understanding to bear on
the significant stories of their own past, or when they might
conceptualize literary techniques and bring conscious artistry to
their fictional narrative writing, many adolescents stop writing
stories at all. They continue to tell them, of course, but teachers
call those stories gossip and cut them off at the bell.

Oral storytelling as a learning medium virtually disappears in
high school, although recent works by teacher-researchers such
as Betty Rosen (1988) and Elizabeth Radin Simons (1990) show
it to be very effective, especially in a culturally diverse classroom. A subtler loss is the narrative conversation that occurs as
part of the writing conference or textbook study. Nancy Martin
has documented the process by which younger children participating in a writing conference use the story at hand as a spring-
board for related narratives from their own experience:

We suggest that the personal 'stories' are in fact the basic fabric of children's conversations, the *means* by which they enter into other people's experiences, try them on for fit and advance into general ideas. It would seem likely that adults also do this, that we, collectively, through anecdotes, build a shared representation of some aspect of life. . . . (1983, 31)

It is this "advance into general ideas" that the school seeks to bring about by requiring the student to produce transactional instead of narrative writing, but Martin's observations suggest that such a requirement goes about the task backwards. General ideas first take shape from a concrete base instead of coming to birth full grown in their final conceptual form.

Conversation, being open-ended and unstructured, is hard to come by in a classroom where the curricular goal is to cover a certain amount of material in a given length of time. In such classrooms, most of the communication is one way only: from teacher to students. It is very easy for a teacher to enter the classroom as the representative of a certain body of knowledge. *Huckleberry Finn* is constant, the form of a thesis paper stays the same, while the students change from year to year. But it is the stream of kids that is most important, simply because they *do* change: they are alive, and it is what they become, and how they apply what they learn — not the specific content of their learning — that will determine how the world carries on. The teacher who emphasizes subject — who presents a novel as a form to be analyzed, and a writing assignment as a structure to be fleshed out with concepts — may meet the curricular objectives but does little to connect her students with the great resources of narrative thought. This teacher does not encourage students to speak and write their own narratives. The story has value only as text, something existing apart from (probably above) the students and their lives, some sanctified dead thing to be observed and studied. On the other hand, the teacher who approaches the stories of her discipline and the personal stories of her students as rich wellsprings of knowledge about life helps students to know themselves and their world.

Narrative in Teaching and Learning

Children face an increasingly complex and difficult world as they grow up. It's confusing, and often not very safe, to be a teenager in America today. High school students need to know all they can about the world and how best they can make their way in it. Narrative serves the adolescent as a powerful medium for this kind of learning in two ways that transactional language cannot.

First, narrative allows adolescents to look back and make sense of their experience. Little children have to take the world on faith, but teenagers can go back in memory to organize and evaluate the events of their childhood. Second, narrative gives them a forum in which to speculate about the future. In story all things are possible. Where transactional language chooses among options and defends one interpretation as preferable to all others, narrative embraces ambiguity. Often teenagers don't yet have sufficient data to make wise choices about issues important to them. By using a combination of their knowledge of the past and their imagination to project in narrative an image of the future, students can try on different shadings of the truth and discover where their own beliefs lie.

I don't mean to imply that adolescents should not be encouraged, guided, and taught to think rationally and write good transactional prose. I'm arguing that they will have a greater chance of succeeding if these cognitive skills grow organically on a base of prior learning. English teachers are all too familiar with the experience of introducing a form (the classic five-paragraph essay, for example) and getting it back empty. The student who still conceives new experiences in terms of story—and that is most students, and probably the teacher as well—will be better able to generalize and conceptualize the underlying ideas if given the opportunity to tell the story first.

Narrative Learning: ON WITH THE STORY in High School and Beyond

Throughout my years of teaching literature and writing, I have become more and more convinced that narrative is an extremely rich learning medium for adolescents. Its forms are intuitive, its applications manifold. The story of whatever the student has experienced rises up naturally to mediate between the experience itself (whether a memory of childhood, a science experiment, a lecture in history, or the reading of someone else's story) and an exposition, a judgment, or an analysis of the event. Story is the mind's first effort to make sense of experience. It is an integrative response that relates thought to feeling and seeks to make connections with other experiences and other learning. To skip over a student's narrative response by requiring him to move straight to exposition, analysis, or argument is to deny the impact of the lesson on the learner; yet this is what many American high school teachers do.

Another compelling reason to keep narrative at the forefront in school is that students, like all human beings, *need* stories. The narrative drive may not be as strong as those other two tyrants of the adolescent psyche, food and sex, but it is nonetheless a force to be reckoned with. I have seen students sit rapt at their computer keyboards right through lunch period; I have even seen them brush off the attentions of an attractive classmate of the opposite sex while in the throes of creating a story. More impressive, I have seen adolescents change their beliefs and behavior in response to great literary narratives. *Romeo and Juliet*, for example, intervenes positively in parent-teenager conflicts; I have had several students confide in their journals that the failure of communication in the Capulet and Montague families prompted them to talk to their own parents.

Language, as Bakhtin points out, is a social instrument; people need to engage in dialogue, to respond to the ideas and stories of others—and they encounter a powerful flow of these in school.

> The fact is that when the listener perceives and understands the meaning (the language meaning) of speech, he simultaneously takes an active, responsive attitude toward it. He either agrees or disagrees with it (completely or partially), augments it, applies it, prepares for its execution, and so on.... Sooner or later what is heard and actively understood will find its response in the subsequent speech or behavior of the listener.... Everything we have said here also pertains to written and read speech.... (1986, 68–69)

My students' narratives resonate with their understandings of what they are in the process of reading and studying in their classes. They convert passive learning into active communication of what has been learned.

The What and Why of Teaching Through Narrative

In this book I propose to call on my personal teaching experience to describe *what* uses of narrative work in the high school classroom and on secondary research to explore *why* they are effective. I want to show that narrative applications go far beyond simply the reading, writing, and telling of stories. They have a significant role to play in the most important issues facing American education today, including the development of badly needed interdisciplinary and multicultural curricula. This is because story transcends the divisions among areas of knowledge, cuts across cultural boundaries, and lays the foundation for literacy itself.

I am arguing that *what* the teachers of adolescents and young adults should do (in all subjects, not just English) is include more narrative—written, spoken, and read—in their lessons. There are three basic reasons *why*. First, their students will learn more willingly and more effectively as a result. Second, the more stories of human behavior those students incorporate into their experience of the world, the better able they will be to make informed, humane choices in their own lives. And third, an infusion of narrative can only improve an educational system that emphasizes the products of learning over the process, a system that thus limits the possibilities for learning by setting restricted goals (ultimately symbolized by the standardized test). The more stories of human behavior adolescents or adults can summon up and apply to a given situation, the more likely they are to deal constructively with the process of working through it.

For teachers who come to agree with my premises and are interested in pursuing their implementation, there are literally thousands of good sources readily available. I urge teachers to adopt whatever works for them. I have included at the end of each chapter a section called "Practical Matters." Each describes a classroom application I have successfully used based upon some idea explored in that chapter. *They are suggestions only.* My classroom practices may or may not work for you; there are many effective ways to include narrative in teaching and learning, and I encourage teachers to explore and experiment for themselves. Any lesson plan that incorporates story is likely to enhance the experience of the learner.

≡ Two

The Nature and the Study
of Narrative Truth

Narrative as a topic of inquiry is enormous. It over-
flows the boundaries of definition and theory. Among human
beings, the ability and the need to tell stories is universal. The
human mind is a great organizer; just as it learns to arrange the
sensory data of shape, size, color, and distance into a "true" picture of the material world, so also it learns to sort through the
massive, undifferentiated data of experience to create the "true"
story of a person's life.

What we *see* is private. My vision of the color maroon, for
example, may be completely different from your vision of
maroon; we have no way of knowing. No medium exists for the
sharing of visions.[1] But what we *experience* may be shared,
through the medium of language. Thus my life story—the
choices I make, the goals I pursue—may well be modified when
I incorporate into it the story of your experience. Vicariously,
through the medium of words, your experience becomes my
own; I can relive it as though I had been there myself, although
some of the details surely will not match, as I project the events
of your life onto the landscape of mine.

Not only can my mind formulate narratives of actual events—
ordering and giving form to particular details from a chaos of
sensations or from the language of someone else—but it is able
through imagination to *create* stories that embody my concept of
what is "true" about human experience. Those with a wide
imagination and a way with words become our authors, our sto-

---

[1] Thanks to one of my students, Henry Pratt, for this idea.

14

rytellers. Often the fictions of the storyteller are so vivid and wise that they seem more "true" than daily life. This is because the storyteller, not being stuck with the accidents and interruptions and grocery lists that clutter actual experience, can select and arrange events in such a way that they seem to make sense.

People crave stories. Human beings learn and grow in their ability to deal with the world when they participate imaginatively in experience shaped by art. Thus narrative "truth" is moral, not objective; every listener is unique, and each derives value from the story according to his or her own needs. I think of *Romeo and Juliet*: my adolescent students, breathlessly caught up in romantic love and societal disapproval, hardly notice the existence of Friar Lawrence, whose dilemma as a teacher/mentor wrings my heart.

Definition and Functions of Narrative

Narrative erupts at the intersection of experience, emotion, and language. To analyze it by separating those elements is artificial, but to approach it holistically seems impossible; the inquirer soon betrays underlying assumptions, whether those of the linguist, psychiatrist, literary critic, learning theorist, sociologist, historian, writer, or teacher. All these people have valid things to say about the nature of narrative. They are not in agreement, though, because within each of the various disciplines narrative serves different purposes. Donald Polkinghorne, a scholar/practitioner in psychology, offers the best general *definition* I have found of narrative; he defines it as

> a scheme by means of which human beings give meaning to their experience of temporality and personal actions. Narrative meaning functions to give form to the understanding of a purpose to life and to join everyday actions and events into episodic units. It provides a framework for understanding the past events of one's life and for planning future actions. It is the primary scheme by means of which human existence is rendered meaningful. (1988, 11)

In his book *Acts of Meaning*, Jerome Bruner limns with broad strokes the many *functions* of narrative:

15

It deals . . . with the stuff of human action and human intentional-ity. It mediates between the canonical world of culture and the more idiosyncratic world of beliefs, desires, and hopes. It renders the exceptional comprehensible and keeps the uncanny at bay. . . . It reiterates the norms of the society without being didactic. And . . . it provides a basis for rhetoric without confrontation. It can even teach, conserve memory, or alter the past. (1990, 52)

I like Bruner's assertion, almost an afterthought, that "it [narra-tive] can even teach." The role of narrative in teaching and learning is what this whole book is about.

Narrative as Process

Our technological culture likes products: objects that can be manipulated, measured, and defined. One problem in pinning down the nature of narrative is that it deals with process, not product. There are products, of course—*Romeo and Juliet*, for example—but the narrative is not the actual book that we hold in our hands. It is a linguistic representation of a series of events that unfold through time. The reality of a story, therefore, lies not in the physical words on the page but in the experience they evoke. Instead of an object that can be manipulated, measured, and defined, a story is an action that takes place in the imagina-tion of the reader or listener.

A narrative is a representation of events in process. At the same time, it calls forth in each reader an imaginative re-creation of those events. The actions themselves don't change—a student once told me she watched the film of *Romeo and Juliet* twice, hoping the second time that Juliet would wake up two minutes earlier, but of course she didn't. Even though the events them-selves remain constant, however, readers do not.

Each reader brings to the play a unique context of cultural and personal knowledge, experience, and expectations. The Eliz-abethan playgoer four hundred years ago and I thirty-some years ago and my students Molly, Ethan, and others two months ago each took the individual voyage to make sense in our own lives of the events in *Romeo and Juliet*,and it was a dif-ferent experience for each of us. Growing up in diverse times and places, being of different sex and cultural background and socioeconomic stratum, each of us envisioned the same dramatic events against the backdrop of a whole different world.

The re-creation of a Shakespearean drama is not like the re-creation of an experiment in chemistry. The chemical reaction remains the same, no matter who conducts the experiment. But narrative has to do with the personal idiosyncrasies of human experience rather than the scientifically observable generalities. It thus involves the processes by which a particular individual within a particular social context discovers meaning in experience.

The Many Faces of Narrative

Another problem in understanding the nature of narrative lies in the fact that it comes in so many guises. For example, are narrative and story the same thing? Kieran Egan (1989, 102) suggests that narrative is a simple unsorted recitation of events, while story has an ending—a purpose in the selection and ordering of detail. But how is one to tell the difference? Often, after reading a student's writing, I'm not sure where it took me, but the journey itself seems to have made sense. Any storyteller makes choices, even though they may seem artless; experience is far too vast and various to be captured whole in words. Therefore I will use the terms *narrative* and *story* interchangeably throughout this book.

Is it justifiable to cite *Romeo and Juliet*, a drama, as an example in discussing narrative? Yes, because drama is the purest form of narrative—story pared down to its essentials. It comes closer than any other linguistic form to the experience it represents. By extension, if a play by Shakespeare is a form of narrative, so also are soap operas, TV sitcoms, and Saturday-morning cartoons. And drama is not the only kind of play built upon narrative; a child manipulating dolls or trucks also structures play by telling the continuously evolving story of the toys.

It is impossible to imagine life without narrative. We are bathed in it constantly. The newspaper narrates the day's events; TV and radio put out a constant stream of drama and news stories; books and songs and phone calls are full of stories, and so is the family conversation over the dinner table. Describing narrative as a "primary act of mind," Barbara Hardy points out that even as adults

> we dream in narrative, daydream in narrative, remember, anticipate, hope, despair, believe, doubt, plan, revise, criticize, construct, gossip, learn, hate, and love by narrative. In order really to live, we make up stories about ourselves and others, about the personal as well as the social past and future. (1977, 12)

Narrative puts on a different face for every occasion. It may take the form of history, a novel, an anecdote, a lie. Also, narrative varies its relationship to reality depending upon the intentions of the teller. Stories may claim to be factual truth at one end of the spectrum or metaphoric truth at the other, with all shadings in between. A story's "truth" depends more upon its coherence than upon its faithfulness to actual events. Myth and fiction are so powerful because they *seem* true. Again to quote Jerome Bruner:

> A ... feature of narrative is that it can be "real" or "imaginary" without loss of its power as a story.... The story's indifference to extralinguistic reality underlines the fact that it has a structure that is internal to discourse. In other words, the sequence of its sentences, rather than the truth or falsity of any of those sentences, is what determines its overall configuration or plot. It is this unique sequentiality that is indispensable to a story's significance and to the mode of mental organization in terms of which it is grasped. (1990, 44)

Narrative in a Literate Culture

I'm concerned primarily with written, as opposed to oral, narrative because American culture (no matter what criticisms are laid at the schoolhouse door) is profoundly literate. The first thing we strive to teach our children when they reach school is how to read and write. Children soon understand from their teachers' emphasis on drill work and rote response that the *how to* is of more immediate concern than the *what*, the content, of the stories shared by the class.

18

In an oral culture, truth is the story itself; in a literate society, truth is too likely to be perceived as technique, the ability to discern and create conventional structures and relationships in language. English as it is taught in American secondary schools and colleges is preoccupied with forms. Most of us serve up, in varying combinations, a smorgasbord of spelling tests and grammar lessons, plot and theme, thesis and argument. This may appear to be a reasonable learning approach in a technological society, which values language foremost as a tool. It does, however, have a profoundly negative effect on the ways in which we regard or shortchange narrative truth. And as our children reach high school age, we too often tend to emphasize formal language skills at the expense of story, thereby losing the power of narrative as a tool for learning. This is a great loss in a society struggling to maintain a vision of human equality and political democracy. Because it seeks to convey the truth of human experience, narrative is a moral art; the lessons we learn from stories make us not only more skilled, but also better people.

School Teachers and Academic Scholars

The ideas in this book arose originally from my experiences as a teacher of adolescents. The research, tied to graduate school courses, came later; and even though I've been blessed with expert guidance from a number of scholars, it has been at best somewhat scattershot. Research has always struck me as something of a game: a mix of rules, strategy, and challenging fun. I believe now, after years of vigorous but unsystematic study, that my somewhat random pursuit of knowledge reflects my personal and professional preferences.

It's a strange thing: although they are deeply involved with learning, and although their goals to establish and disseminate truth ostensibly coincide, the public high school teacher and the academic professor are more often than not quite different in their approach to knowledge. The differences are both practical and philosophical. *Both teachers serve the pursuit of truth.* It is in the techniques with which they pursue and communicate knowledge that college and high school teachers characteristically differ, and the differences reflect the population of those whom they serve.

In practice, academic scholars tend to be elitist and exclusionary. It is their task to separate: to carve knowledge into areas of expertise and prove that their arguments are more valid than those of other scholars. They serve a truth that transcends the limited world view of those whom they teach. Public school teachers, on the other hand, are ideally democratic and eclectic. They have a vested interest in behaving this way, because it is their job to accept and believe in the potential of every student who shows up in their classroom. They are used to trying a thousand different things in their attempt to meet the vast array of needs and learning styles their students bring to them. An American public high school teacher is more likely to respond to the concrete needs of a hurting human being in her second-period class than to an abstract generalization of human behavior drawn from chapter two of the book under study.

Public school teachers are often described as being "in the trenches" of education. This is an apt analogy not just for their relationship to learners, but for their relationship to knowledge. Public high school teachers do not have the privilege of theorizing and strategizing about truth with an elite corps of learners. They grab the standard issue, whatever it may be — a dogeared text, a mixed-bag anthology, a flickery old TV set — and plunge into the fray.

The Relationship of Research to Practice

As a public classroom teacher engaged in secondary research, I found it very difficult to choose one theoretical stance over another. My instincts led me to ask not so much which approach was *right* as what insight each new approach had to offer. Also, my patience with theory went just so far. I much prefer research designed to be directly applicable to the students I meet every day. Therefore I feel more sympathy with scholars such as Vygotsky, Bakhtin, and Britton, who seek to integrate language, learning, communication, and human development, than with those such as Saussure, Chomsky, and Halliday, who deal with language as a discrete system of signs independent of its users. I particularly appreciate researchers such as Wertsch (1991), Nelson (1989), and Brandt (1992), whose recent works build on the valid findings of both these strands of thought. Although their tone is academic, they do seek, in the words of Wertsch, "a more general perspective." He articulates the need, with which I heartily concur, to "create units of analysis that work against the tendency toward disciplinary fragmentation and isolation" (4).

It's paradoxical that to come to a better understanding of the nature and uses of narrative, which is itself intuitive and integrative, I found myself reading the literature of scholarly research, which is cognitive and analytical. I was slogging through a jargon-laden but valuable paper when Huckleberry Finn's comment about *Pilgrim's Progress* floated unbidden into my mind: "I read considerable in it from time to time. The statements was interesting, but tough" (Twain 1958, 130). As Huck, a voyager living his spiritual journey from day to day, found both fascination and difficulty in Bunyan's guide book to redemption, so I, a teacher living every day with the language and stories of young people, found both fascination and difficulty in books about linguistic theory and cognitive growth.

Of course, being eclectic, I wandered happily off into byways of cultural criticism, theory of genre, literary analysis, interdisciplinary studies, autobiography, myth and folklore, journal keeping, and who knows what else. Here were other scholars with broader perspectives to appreciate, authors such as Jerome Bruner, Raymond Williams, Robert Coles, Joseph Campbell. They all have important things to say. I even found significant material in my husband's high-tech computer literature. The realms of narrative are numberless; that's one of the reasons it makes a universal base for learning.

Narrative in the Real Lives of Teachers and Adolescents

I make no claims to scholarship. I am by training and by choice a public school teacher. My classroom practice, limited primarily to one middle school by Lake Champlain and one junior/

senior high school in the foothills of Vermont's Green Mountains, is as individual and particular — and as universal—as good narrative. The students whose works I quote are not generic teenagers; they are real flesh-and-blood kids from every social subset and every academic level of the schools in which I have taught, and they are very dear to me. From them I have learned many truths:

Through narrative, adolescents can imaginatively experience the lives of other peoples and other centuries. By telling their own stories, these adolescent learners validate the deepest, most significant experiences in their own lives. They can come to grips with the themes and questions common to all human beings. They can keep alive a child's joy in creativity while developing an adult's cognitive capabilities. They can make connections through metaphor and distinctions through detail. They can make the transition, through story, from sensory data to generalized concept. They can explore, adopt, modify, or reject the genres of their culture, developing their personal values and communication skills in the process. Furthermore, most of them will take some pride and pleasure in doing these worthwhile things. To share stories is academically sound practice — and it's also fun.

Practical Matters

My students have a favorite narrative game, one that my family has enjoyed since I can remember. I first introduced it to my classes with some trepidation, because actually it's a lot of work, but the students beg to play — including most of those who generally perceive themselves to be poor writers.

I break the class into groups of equal size, each containing both boys and girls, both scholars and strugglers, because it goes better that way. Seven seems to be the optimum number, but groups from five to eight work well. The game may be played at a circle of desks or a row of computers. Everyone is supplied with plenty of paper and pencils or a disk. I join the group containing the most likely saboteurs.

Before starting, I introduce the concept of popular genre. After identifying several types — horror, fairy tale, and Western, for example—I ask the students to name others, which they do readily. Then each player privately chooses a genre.

The directions for play come next: "You will have four minutes [more or less, depending on the size of the groups and the length of the period] to begin a story in the genre of your choice. In those four minutes you must establish your genre, your main character, the main character's conflict, and the setting. At the end of four minutes I will say, 'Pass!' at which point you must *immediately* stop writing and pass your paper to the person on your right [or move to the computer on your right].

"At this point you have to change in a hurry, because it's your job to continue the story now in front of you. Suppose Justin, here, started a tender romance, but when he gets Kim's story he finds it's a bloodthirsty horror tale. Justin has to let the romance go and write like Stephen King. In the meantime, Kim gets Laurie's paper and finds she has to shift from horror to a cute little kid's story with talking rabbits. The point is to write effectively in each new genre.

"Every four minutes I'll say 'Pass!' and you'll get someone else's story until we've gone around the group. It's the last person's responsibility to end the story. You may have as much time as you need to finish, and then pass it along so the person who started it can read it.

"Two rules: keep it clean and have fun."

In the language of the sixties, this game is "a happening." Some of the stories work—sort of—and most of them don't, but the value lies in the process, not the product. Few things so totally absorbing ever happen in a classroom. The scratch of pencils, the click of keys are the only sounds as the players race time to complete their segment of each story. Occasionally someone, reading a new story in preparation to write, more or less successfully smothers a laugh. But at the end of the class period, when the stories are completed and shared with the group, hilarity reigns. The authors can't wait to see what happened to this character or how someone got out of that situation.

I enjoy this game as much as my students do. For one thing, it's an ideal vehicle for introducing the concept of genre. Also,

23

by demanding active participation toward a common goal, it bonds classmates who ordinarily would disdain the opportunity to work together (in my family gatherings, it has bonded branch with branch, and old with young). Finally, it asks young students of literature to gnaw pleasurably on the very bones of literary endeavor. And, to be honest, I want as much as they do to find out what happened to the character I launched in the beginning.

≡ Three

Myth and Magic

Matt had been sent to the office, and he was angry. He folded his lanky frame into a too-small desk, glared at the windowless, drab little room reserved for miscreants, then dug into his book bag for his journal. "I can't stand math," he wrote in large firm script.

It was quiet in the office and there was nothing else to do, so after a seething pause, Matt continued writing. "It's too bad that Ms. B. hasn't missed a day of school in about 8 years. I sometimes wish that something would happen to her so I would never see her again."

The pencil whispered across the page, the room disappeared, and gradually Matt's scowl tipped up into a smile as he pursued his gentle revenge:

I wish a rift would open up and some strange aliens with big noses would abduct her and bring her to another planet and teach her how to skate board. Then maybe she would be a little more laid back and not constantly getting me in trouble. . . .

Maybe I'll get a dog and teach it how to talk. I would spend all my spare time to teach my dog how to talk. Then once it could talk, I would tell it to go over to Ms. B's house and have a conversation. I would have him tell Ms. B. not to ever get me in trouble again or he would eat all of her cats. I bet she wouldn't get me in trouble again.

Another thing I wish I could do was to go to Afghanistan and become their king. Then I would come back to the U.S. and buy a game show. Then I would come to Bristol, have a lottery in which the prize was a ticket to the game show and have Ms. B. win. Then

I would have her win the game show, in which the prize was a vacation in Beautiful Afghanistan. Then I would give her a tour guide and have him tell her to do something that would be against the law. Then I would exile her from Afghanistan and ruin her vacation.

I could also take a 50 lb. bag of potato*es* (Dan Quayle was here) and leave it on her porch. Then when she saw them, she would take them inside and try to cook them, but she wouldn't be able to because they would all be rubber. Ha Ha Ha! Now *that* would be funny. . . .

It would also be really funny if the aliens that taught Ms. B. how to skate board gave her two bags of potatoes. The first bag that they gave her would be real and when she went to eat the second bag, they were rubber! Or maybe if I sent my talking dog over pulling a wagon with a 50 lb. bag of potatoes. Then those would be rubber too!

Another thing I could do is to use my mom's crockpot to make some beef stew. Then while it was still warm, I would bring it over as a peace offering. Then I would leave. When she sat down to eat the stew, she would find out that the potatoes in it were rubber!

— *Matt, 16*

Stories as Magic

Stories are magic — that's the single most important thing to remember about them. From Santa Claus and the tooth fairy to the neutron and Godot, we use the medium of narrative to invoke those mysterious potent entities that we know exist because we can imagine them. Caged in the back room of the office, Matt appears powerless against the authority of his math teacher; but given pencil, paper, and an inspired burst of imagination, he conjures up a menagerie of talking dogs and big-nosed aliens and Afghanistanians to bring her to her just desserts.

"The idea," says Matt, "was to get even without hurting her."

Like most stories that call on the supernatural — myths, fairy and folk tales, religious parables and fables — Matt's fantasy is supremely moral. Storytellers constantly struggle with the conflict between the way things *are* and the way things *ought to be*.

Some storytellers, such as the nameless mythmakers of the past, call on imagination to explain a reality for which there is no obvious cause or justification. Others, like Matt, deliberately free themselves from the constraints of representing a tangible reality in order to improve upon it. Both of these are moral stances; in each case the storyteller is treating the world responsibly, by attempting either to render it comprehensible or to right its perceived wrongs.

Matt, at sixteen, does not *believe* in his aliens or his talking dog. Indeed, his whole fantasy is couched in the subjunctive: this or that *would* happen. But his creatures are both real and satisfying to him as he *creates* them. He has no trouble still tapping into the sort of magical mood that sustains a child through bad moments. It is easy to forget, as we grow older and our supply of information accretes and hardens, how fluid and myriad are the possibilities available to youth. Young children do not make distinctions between fact and fantasy. All the ways of the world are new to them, and they spend virtually all their time trying to determine, by whatever means possible—very often by means of storytelling—both how things are and how they ought to be.

The Power of Magic in Adolescence

Magic still holds tremendous power in the lives of adolescents. During the middle school years, syncretic thinking begins to give way to more cognitive processes, but it doesn't happen overnight. The shift is gradual, and often two ways of conceptualizing exist side by side in the same developing mind. The adolescent stands one foot in each camp between the enchantment of a child's world and the rationality of an adult's. I remember when one seventh grader looked up, somewhat dazed, after a period of intense silent reading. Clutching a battered copy of Tolkein's *The Two Towers* and frowning in puzzlement at the familiar classroom, he told me, "I'm more at home in Middle Earth than I am here."

Fully sensible but still uninitiated, adolescents occupy a spot in their personal growth that parallels the place of mythmakers and fabulists in the development of knowledge. These wise, faceless figures observe events that defy sensory logic. Through their stories, they mediate through the ages between primitive man's wonder in the face of inexplicable nature and the scientist's rational approach to describing it. For them, as for children, reality encompasses the possibilities conceived by imagination; they shape their world through art, and thus endow it with purpose and a human ethic.

Early teenagers are irresistibly drawn to myth and fairy tale, folklore and legend. Generally speaking, these are tales without authors, forged through generations of retellings and shaped by the fundamental rhythms of human life, not by the inventions of an individual. As they grow older, many students, yearning still to validate the magic that stirs within them despite a culture that denies it, will add the more modern and more consciously crafted epic, adventure fantasy, and science fiction to their list of preferred genres. In a way it seems irresponsible to lump together the grandeur of myth with the lesser fabulous genres, but myth informs all the others. Bill Moyers tells us that even such a renowned expert as Joseph Campbell, on seeing the film *Star Wars*, "reveled in the ancient themes and motifs of mythology unfolding on the wide screen in powerful contemporary images" (Campbell 1988, xiii). Campbell, in fact, spent much effort sharing the presence and relevance of myth in modern western culture and loved teaching it: "Young people just grab this stuff. Mythology teaches you what's behind literature and the arts, it teaches you about your own life. It's a great, exciting, life-nourishing subject" (1988, 14).

The Fabulous Genres as a Learning Medium

Most middle and high school students are so well grounded in the narrative forms of folk and fairy tale that they can read and write these and related genres with considerable sophistication. Thus these tales represent an ideal medium for learning. There are no facts or figures in a fairy tale, no experimental data in a myth, no literary realism in a fable; therefore some teachers consider these forms too childish for high school students. But there is still a lot of the child in adolescents. They are at the ideal age to be taught, explicitly, that there are many pathways to truth and many ways of knowing. And, as Bruno Bettelheim makes clear in his defense of the folk fairy tale,

> a child needs to understand what is going on within his conscious self so that he can also cope with that which goes on in his unconscious. He can achieve this understanding, and with it the ability to cope, not through rational comprehension of the nature and content of his unconscious, but by becoming familiar with it through spinning out daydreams — ruminating, rearranging, and fantasizing about suitable story elements in response to unconscious pressures. By doing this, the child fits unconscious content into conscious fantasies, which then enable him to deal with that content. (1977, 7)

I often introduce an excursion into one of the "magic" genres by asking students to discuss daydreams, sometimes in conjunction with a reading of Thurber's classic story, "The Secret Life of Walter Mitty." I've never yet met a ninth grader who would not confess to fantasizing stories, and most enjoy engaging in conjecture about the underlying pressures that shape their daydreams. Adolescents intuitively understand the magical aspects of daydreaming, even when there are no monsters or talking animals involved. It is magical to create a world out of nothing but what Dick Francis termed "the illuminations crashing about in my head" (1990, 5). They comprehend also the relationship between daydreaming and storytelling. Myth and folk genres are popular with adolescents because they bring together in an accessible format all these elements: magic, daydreaming, and storytelling. Even more important, they explore across cultures and through centuries the most basic moral values, "not through abstract ethical concepts but through that which seems tangibly right and therefore meaningful . . . " (Bettelheim 1977, 5).

Given the choice, most middle and high school students would rather write fiction than any other linguistic form. Especially in response to literature, and most particularly fabulous literature, teenagers overflow with stories; their daydreams and their moral questionings, often unwelcome in the school setting, are validated by the artistic models before them. It is perfectly appropriate to ask students to respond to myth by becoming mythmakers. Adults tend to cut teenagers off from their creativity the way they cut them off from their feelings: "Big boys/girls don't cry," and by the same token, "Big boys/girls don't write fantasies." Most adolescents survive all right—even if they stumble onto knowledge as a dry turf, without the mediation of narrative understanding and emotional involvement—but something important is lost.

Adolescents suffer a lot; it comes with the territory. While teachers are typically sensitive to this, they also typically deny it, trying to move kids beyond "silliness" or "immaturity" to more rational responses to instruction. It is an endless balancing act. No teacher can truly know and cherish 115 kids a day; it's a task impossible to achieve, but vital to attempt. Here, myth and folk/fairy fiction are a teacher's ally. Within their safe boundaries teenagers are able to bring their anxieties to a happy ending, as in the fairy tale; or understand that their suffering is heroic and purposeful, as in a myth; or define and explore the moral imperatives of their society, as in a folk tale.

Magic, Art, and Morality: The Adolescent as Fabulist and Mythmaker

Teenagers are wonderful mythmakers for two reasons. The first is that enough of the child remains to find the lure and metaphoric truths of magic very strong, yet enough of the adult has developed to create sophisticated narrative structures. The second reason is more complicated; it has to do with both the timeless nature of myth itself and the naive idealism of adolescence. For the most part, young people are not taken with subtleties. They are interested in tackling the biggest questions of human life in language that is immediately meaningful to themselves. Therefore they fit very well Berthoff's most helpful and perceptive description of the mythmaker:

> But to be a mythmaker, to move toward myth, is not simply to invent new fictions, including exploratory or ironic reconstructions

of famous individual myths. It is rather to compose by way of continuously refreshing the substance of what people characteristically say in each other's presence up and down the whole range, or some great part of it, of purposeful human utterance. (1970, 286)

Teenagers relish the challenge of "refreshing the substance" of what people say about fundamental human issues. No perspective is fresher or more purposeful than that of adolescents. When the utterances of mythmakers or fabulists come into their presence, they enter into dialogue. My students have engaged with many myths and folk tales, including the well-known ancient myths of Egypt and Greece; lesser-known tales from cultures about which they were learning in global studies, such as Russian and Indian; creation myths from around the world; and holiday myths.

The openness of fabulous fiction is welcome to a young author whose moral views are likely still to be ambivalent, still in the process of formation. For a student who is wrestling with questions of right and wrong, authority and individual will, the movement from one stage of life to another, it is very helpful to have a familiar, culturally sanctioned narrative form in which to engage the issues. Writing is a multilayered discipline; insight comes more readily when structural matters are under control. It has been shown that when writers are grappling with ideas, they have more trouble with the technical and formal aspects of writing (Brannon 1985). The more comfortable young writers are with their genre, the better they are able to formulate and express their thoughts. And because the themes matter deeply to them, they bring to bear all the artistic means at their disposal in order to make the stories communicate their truths effectively.

Often my students are driven by their narratives. I remember an older boy named Tracey who did not think of himself as much of a writer; he had signed up for Creative Writing just to get the last credit necessary to graduate. Several weeks into the semester, after some early struggles, I was pleased to see him absorbed and working hard for three days in a row at the computer keyboard. Toward the end of the third day he raised his hand in distress. "I've got a *problem*."

"What's the matter, Tracey?"

"My character won't do what he's supposed to. He's supposed to die, see, and he doesn't want to!"

In fiction, especially fabulous narrative such as the adventure
fantasy Tracey was writing, the internal coherence of the story
may lead the author to truths he wasn't aware he knew.
Tracey's character (also, significantly, named Tracey) was right
to protest against arbitrary death; true, he had lost his love
(named after Tracey's girlfriend), but as drawn in the story, he
was too heroic a figure not to fight back. The conscious and the
subconscious Tracey were vying for space on the page as the
author was "ruminating, rearranging, and fantasizing about suit-
able story elements" (Bettelheim 1977, 7). In the end, both
author and character (not to mention readers) were better satisfied when the hero survived.

Tracey's character stayed alive because to give up would have
been inconsistent with his code of moral behavior; it would have
been *wrong* for him to die. It is the most profound questions of
right and wrong that myths and folk tales address, the questions
we all must answer for our own selves, in the context of our own
time and culture, in order to be able to live harmoniously in the
world. And this idea leads to another important reason for cul-
tivating myth in the classroom. In a multicultural and democratic society, such a powerful means of promoting harmonious
living is worth cherishing.

Myth and the Democratic Ideal

Berthoff sees myth as an antidote to prejudice:

> Myth is open and absorptive narrative thinking, generous by defini-
> tion — and the strongest cultural obstacle to the murderous narrowing
> down of fictitious explanation represented by anti-Semitism or by
> race and class hatred of any kind is the persistence and extension of
> myth, so understood. In these terms the ultimate justification of
> pluralistic (as opposed to merely egalitarian) democracy would be
> that it contributes better than other civil systems to this persistence.
> (1970, 283)

Because myth as a way of knowing cuts across cultural boundaries to touch us at the levels of our shared humanity, teenagers

involved in reading and writing fabulous literature are also involved in discovering their commonalities. They are taking upon themselves the authority to make a "purposeful human utterance" about how to live in the world. Joseph Campbell believes that granting this authority to ordinary people, including schoolchildren, is inherent to living in a democracy. Describing the symbolic meaning of the Great Seal of the United States, he points out that "from above or below, or from any point of the compass, the creative Word might be heard, which is the great thesis of democracy. Democracy assumes that anybody from any quarter can speak, and speak truth, because his mind is not cut off from the truth" (1988, 35).

The Teenager, the Fable, and the Pursuit of Truth

In the fabulous narratives of middle and high school students there are many truths to be found, and a good deal of their power lies in their artistic achievement. Several years ago my eighth-grade class read a number of myths and a small collection of Aesop's fables. One member of the class, a thirteen-year-old girl named Keely, wrote the following little fable, which I found stunning. I want to look at this story with some care, because it shows so clearly a profound moral struggle, complex narrative skill, and the relationship between them.

The Dove and the Crow

Once a long time ago there was a white dove more beautiful and clean than freshly fallen snow itself. It flew over and around its mountain every morning at eight a.m., looking for its breakfast: olives, grapes, and raspberries. Every bird in the valley admired and cherished this beautiful bird.

There was an ugly black crow who especially loved her and wanted her as his bride. But the beautiful bird had no intention of ever liking this disgusting crow and totally ignored him.

This made the crow very angry, and he got very jealous of all the white male doves that the beautiful dove talked to. So one night the envious crow went out and bought seven black coals. He marked all over the white male doves and made them as black as himself.

33

The next day, when the gorgeous bird went out to hunt for breakfast, all she saw was a bunch of ugly black crows. So she went up to any one of the black beasts (which happened to be the crow) and started talking to him.

All went well from then on for the crow, but the dove was never really happy again.

— Keely, 13

"The Dove and the Crow" rewards study because it clearly illustrates both the kinds of value conflicts that are vital to young adolescents and the narrative artistry, whether conscious or unconscious, that they are able to employ in their explorations of values. Keely's sequencing of events and her choice of vocabulary show that she understands the fable as a narrative form, but they go deeper than form to a more personal level of understanding. The most important aspect of this fable is that its lesson or "moral" is ambiguous; this ambiguity is intentional and is artistically achieved.

The story succeeds as a fable because it correctly uses the conventions of fable. The characters are animals treated anthropomorphically and stereotypically to represent generalized human characteristics. (Keely's symbolic use of black and white extends the stereotyping beyond general traits [i.e., a fox is sly] to general values [i.e., black is bad and white is good]. One of the implicit open-ended questions in her paper is about the validity of such stereotyping.) The events of the story arise from the traits of the characters and lead the reader to a conclusion (in this case, more than one possible conclusion) about the consequences of those traits. The language is "fabulous" in its brevity, attention to detail, and resonance.

At the start of the fable, the dove is defined by her whiteness. She is not only beautiful but "clean," an interesting word choice implying both purity of character and virginity. She is also implicitly better than the other birds; the mountain and the exotic foods on it are hers; the other birds literally look up from the valley below to admire her—but they also "cherish" her, which suggests that they view her with some sense of ownership. She is a royal figure at the start of the fable, remote and

34

shining but also in some unspecified way the property of the common birds.

It is an ugly black crow who aspires to marry the dove—not, significantly, one of the male doves. In the second paragraph we see that black is exactly equal to ugly (as white is to beautiful). For narrative purposes, Keely has accepted this stereotype. But then she makes an important shift in viewpoint: it is not the narrator's point of view, but the dove's, that the black crow is "disgusting." Keely's language is very strong here; it would be easy to say simply that the dove didn't like the crow, but indeed she "had no intention of ever liking" him—her dislike was a deliberate choice. By ignoring him, the dove reinforces the image of her own superiority as drawn in the first paragraph. The crow's intentions are presented as honorable; he loves her and wants to marry her. This may be presumptuous, but it does not merit such contempt.

The third paragraph belongs to the crow. We see that he is both angry at the dove for her behavior and jealous of the male doves with whom she talks. These male doves are faceless and comparatively spineless; at no point do they vie with the crow for the dove's affections. They are an avian upper class, accepting the dove's attentions as their prerogative. It's important to note that their "whiteness" is totally effaced by an application of coal and is therefore external, a matter of appearances. Or at least this is the dove's perception—on this point as on many others the reader is left uncertain at the end. In any case, the crow, when he decides to take action, buys not a bucket of whitewash to change himself, but "seven black coals" with which to besmirch the male doves. In a way there is the strong sense that he is bringing them down to his level instead of trying to raise himself to theirs; but in a way he is the more to be admired, because he is the active one while they are passive, and because he remains true to himself. He never pretends to be anything but a crow.

In the fourth paragraph, the language Keely uses to describe the dove undergoes a subtle but potent shift. The dove is no longer beautiful, but *gorgeous*; she *hunts* for breakfast instead of looking for it. Her image is suddenly less like a princess and more like a female predator. The dove, undiscriminating, sees only "a bunch of ugly black crows," and the blackened male doves do not attempt to disabuse her. At this point the dove makes a vitally important choice: "So she went up to any one of the black beasts (which happened to be the crow) and started talking to him." The dove does not have to do this; she can retain her snow-white purity by ignoring all the "crows" as she has ignored the one crow who sought her favor. She is clearly debasing herself by talking to a "beast," but apparently it is more important to her to have someone to whom to talk (note: *to*, not *with*) than to maintain her lofty position. The narrative would lead us to believe that she chooses the crow at random, but by now the reader can imagine that the enterprising crow would have no trouble placing himself in the most likely position to receive her attention.

The end of this fable is a shocker: "All went well from then on for the crow, but the dove was never really happy again." Keely chooses to end abruptly with a variation of the fairy tale formula that "they all lived happily ever after" rather than with the fable's traditional moral. I consider the ending to be valid because Keely is both recognizing and questioning stereotypical values in her society. She does not draw a "moral." Both of her main characters, the dove and the crow, have already been required to choose between alternatives either of which would be possible to them. It is up to the reader to decide what moral is most appropriate. Does the dove suffer because she has not lived up to the standards of whiteness, or because she snobbishly persists in thinking of herself as better than ordinary? Does the crow triumph because he remains true to himself, or because he is a crass social climber, or because he is insensitive to the needs of the one he loves? Keely does not judge; she is still learning, through the art and the magic of story, what is true for her.

Practical Matters

Fabulous stories generally need dialogue — Keely's is unusual in being effective without it. Most young adolescents are able to create lively conversations among their characters, but many are still shaky when it comes to the mechanics of writing them down. Therefore, before the seventh or eighth graders embark upon writing their fabulous tales, I pull out my critterbox and give them a day of practice in the craft of writing dialogue correctly.

The critterbox is just a shoe box into which I toss pictures cut from old magazines or calendars. There are birds and beasts of every sort, photographs of people in unusual clothes or situations, and various cartoon characters. Without looking, each student draws two pictures from the box and creates a brief dialogue (including both conversation and narrative) between the "critters" she has chosen. (Depending on the class, I may choose two pictures also and model the exercise on the blackboard.) Students edit each other's rough drafts; any questions that they can't resolve are brought to me. When the punctuation and paragraphing are perfect on the rough draft, the young writer creates a final draft in ink, glues her "critters" artistically to the paper, and tacks the finished product up on the bulletin board.

This is an old lesson plan; it did not originate with me, and I forget where I first read or saw it many years ago. It's kind of hokey, but it keeps resurfacing because it works—the kids have fun, they do seem to learn the mechanics of writing dialogue, and the bulletin board looks great.

≡Four

Storytelling

As with any generation
the oral tradition depends upon each person
listening and remembering a portion
and it is together —
all of us remembering what we have heard together —
that creates the whole story
the long story of the people.
                                        — *Silko 1981, 6–7*

Western culture took its first great step toward literacy about three thousand years ago, just after the era of Homer, when the Greeks began to utilize the phonetic script of the Phoenician traders. The pictographic script that preceded the Phoenician alphabet, consisting of thousands of word symbols, was very difficult to learn. Thus reading and writing were privileged skills belonging only to the scholarly and the powerful. With the introduction of a writing system that used symbols representing the sounds in words, rather than pictorial representations of the words themselves, reading and writing entered the world of the common man (Zachmann 1991).

In the early days of ancient Greece, words were instruments of the oracle and bard; they built a beautiful foundation of myths on which the culture thrived. As literacy spread and gave rise to an educated upper class, words became the vehicle of a new social concept: democracy. By the time the Greek civilization had given over to Rome, words were tools of practical men who used them to design battles, roadways, or scientific systems. With the spread of literacy, most of the characteristics of an oral culture have been lost to Western civilization.

The Differing Roles of Story in Oral and Literate Cultures

Oral cultures (which still far outnumber literate cultures in today's world) are essentially self-contained, conservative, and land-based. The people are hunters or farmers, dependent upon and closely attuned to earth's natural rhythms. They do not need writing for history, because their sense of time is cyclical rather than linear and progressive. Nor do they need writing for commerce, having no trade, nor for science, having no desire to control or modify the natural world that sustains them. The stories they develop reflect this kinship with nature. These stories are passed down from generation to generation; they belong to a society, not to an author. They give continuity and stability to a culture, preserving traditions and values, at the same time modifying themselves, as all language modifies itself, to adapt to current conditions.

In an oral culture stories are sacred. They explain metaphorically why the world is the way it is; thus the storyteller is a powerful figure, a teller of truth, mouthpiece of the gods. Story in an oral culture leaves no residue or artifact such as symbols on a page; when it "is not actually being told, all that exists of it is the potential in certain human beings to tell it" (Ong 1982, 11). The humble experiences of everyday human life derive meaning from myth.

In a literate culture, however, written communication accumulates. Ordinary people record the how and why of their lives, and gradually these little narratives take on the weight of evidence. Instead of deriving meaning from myth, these experiences themselves become the raw material from which meaning is derived. The stories of individuals become data for the scientist or historian. Narrative is separated from explanation, thereby losing its mystique; it takes its place among the arts, respected, but removed from the center. In a literate culture, including that of our schools, exposition and analysis are seen as higher level language skills and are thus valued above story. But it is still at the level of story that significant learning begins. It is still within stories that culture replenishes itself and values grow.

Literate Culture and the Loss of Shared Experience

As societies develop literacy, they lose the positive qualities of an oral culture. By learning methods to control nature, they give up their close identity with the land—sometimes, sadly, to the point of abusing it, like the late Romans, or like us. They also lose their storytellers, those who have the magical ability to connect with and exalt the everyday experience of a people. Walter Benjamin laments these losses in his great essay, "The Storyteller," written after World War I, in which he observes that a Western culture given over to war and politics has ceased to value personal experience:

> Less and less frequently do we encounter people with the ability to tell a tale properly. More and more often there is embarrassment all around when the wish to hear a story is expressed. It is as if something that seemed inalienable to us, the securest among our possessions, were taken from us: the ability to exchange experiences. . . .

For never has experience been contradicted more thoroughly than strategic experience by tactical warfare, economic experience by inflation, bodily experience by mechanical warfare, moral experience by those in power. A generation that had gone to school on a horse-drawn streetcar now stood under the open sky in a countryside in which nothing remained unchanged but the clouds, and beneath these clouds, in a field of force of destructive torrents and explosions, was the tiny, fragile human body. (1969, 83–84)

In Benjamin's view, it is as though the social changes that accompanied the rise of literacy in Western culture amounted to a loss of Eden. No doubt he would be even more horrified by the world today, a world in which personal experience is continually sucked up by the interpreters of data. It's easy to perceive in the language of our leaders — whether political, economic, military, or religious — that the people of our culture have lost the ability to speak with moral authority; nor is there much beauty or wisdom in their words. In Silko's Laguna Indian community, everyone had the responsibility to listen well and to speak well. The survival of their world depended upon spoken stories, and the children learned from infancy to listen, remember, and retell. In today's dominant Western civilization, this responsibility has yielded to the authority of news briefs, sitcoms, and pollsters.

Written and Spoken Language as Different Ways of Knowing

In school our children learn the skills of reading and writing almost to the exclusion of listening and speaking. In the early grades they may share a bit of show and tell, but by adolescence most learning has been removed from the live arena to the printed page. The listening our high school students do is largely a matter of gathering facts and following directions. They are lucky to speak at all, apart from the high stress requirement to answer questions correctly. When teenagers do speak of their own volition in the classroom, their language is usually spontaneous and expressive, whether in teacher-sanctioned discussion or illicit gossip. It is as though all the talking adolescents do in school is rough draft; they are very seldom asked to shape and polish a verbal utterance. Unpracticed in the skills of public speaking and suspicious of the models available to them, many adolescents are terrified to stand up in front of an audience and talk. The ability to listen critically and to speak with authority is far down on the American public school's practical list of priorities.

Yet, as Halliday makes clear, speaking and listening skills are just as important as reading and writing skills to the learner,

> *because they are different ways of knowing.*
> The written language presents a SYNOPTIC view. It defines its universe as product rather than as process. Whether we are talking about a triangle, the layout of a house, or the organisation of a society, the written language encodes it as a structure . . . as a *thing* that *exists*. In principle we can freeze it, attend to it, and take it in as a whole. . . .
> The spoken language presents a DYNAMIC view. It defines its universe primarily as process, encoding it not as a structure but as constructing — or demolishing. In the spoken language, phenomena do not exist; they *happen*. They are seen as coming into being, changing, moving in and out of focus, and as interacting in a continuous onward flow. (1989, 97, emphasis in original)

"Go with the flow," my students tell each other when life seems to keep them bumping into brick walls. There is very little flow in high school, where learning is full of *things* that *exist*, like triangles.

Recapturing the Flow:
Storytelling in the Classroom

One way English teachers can introduce a little flow for their students is to open up the world of the storyteller. There are good models of storytellers on tape and records; my favorite is Garrison Keillor, whose Lake Wobegon tales manage to sound rambling and purposeful, fanciful and true, comical and wise all at once. Most communities have their own local storytellers who show up at fairs and gatherings and who are happy to entertain schoolchildren. But the best source of good oral stories for a class is right there in the classroom. We all have our own stories to tell, our own unique set of forebears and life experiences. Teachers like Rosen (1988) and Simons (1990) show how to tap into the rich variety of tales and folklore bubbling just under the surface in a multicultural classroom. Sharing and comparing stories, these students develop a voice strengthened by the context of their heritage. All students can participate in a round of personal storytelling; several of my mainstreamed marginal readers have found their niche in the classroom culture by telling tales.

Sometimes, students who have difficulty speaking in their own voice are able to recite the words or paraphrase the ideas of another. The material of the storyteller in an oral culture is old and has been told many times, with variations that are the stamp of the teller. My ninth graders read and tell each other myths and tales from other cultures. When they read excerpts from the *Odyssey*, for example, many choose as a project to learn and retell one of the stories we have not read as a group, and some memorize passages from the Fitzgerald translation. They learn valuable lessons about rhetoric, oral culture, and themselves.

I remember Eli, bright-eyed and vigorous, a born storyteller, telling his rapt classmates the story of Circe: "See she kind of liked Odysseus and she wanted to keep him there, on her island, so you'll never guess what she did! Seriously! She turned his men into *pigs*! And Odysseus was so freaked, he goes, 'Yo, Circe!' He goes, 'What is it with all these *pigs*!'"

Another student, Brahma, memorized and mesmerizingly recited the whole story of Odysseus's visit to the land of the dead, hundreds of lines of iambic pentameter. One of her classmates said afterward, "Did you notice her eyes? Wild! She was looking like right at us, but she couldn't see us. Do you think Homer was *really* blind, or was he just looking at the story in his head?"

The Rewards of Literacy

We can give our students glimpses of the kinds of wisdom inherent in an oral culture, along with more confidence as speakers and more appreciation as listeners; but they will remain the products and practitioners of a literate culture, and this is as it should be. It's easy to romanticize a life of harmony with the earth and wisdom through story. In our world today, such societies are endangered by those more powerful, and they need to become literate in order to survive. Paradoxically, as people gain power through the growth of written knowledge, they give up their important role as the central figures and interpreters of the world. But although the people of an oral culture lose their sustaining myths with the rise of written language, they also gain a great deal:

> Oral cultures indeed produce powerful and beautiful verbal performances of high artistic and human worth, which are no longer even possible once writing has taken possession of the psyche. Nevertheless, without writing, human consciousness cannot achieve its fuller potentials, cannot produce other beautiful and powerful creations. In this sense, orality needs to produce and is destined to produce writing. Literacy ... is absolutely necessary for the development not only of science but also of history, philosophy, explicative understanding of literature and of any art, and indeed for the explanation of language (including oral speech) itself. (Ong 1982, 14–15)

The Thrust of Oral Culture into the Literature of Today

It is possible that the students of this generation will have far more access to the wisdom and values of oral cultures than did their parents. Contemporary literary critics such as Terry Eagleton and Raymond Williams set forth the premise that the literature of a culture shifts and develops organically, along with the culture itself, in a continuous interplay with historic events. If this is so, one of the most interesting developments now occurring in English-American literature is the increasing inclusion of works written by authors born into nonliterate cultures. These works challenge the narrative conventions of both oral tradition and Western literature. To capture the words of spoken story and pin them in print on a page is like capturing a bird from the air and putting it in a cage. They're the same words and the same bird, but our perception of what they are has shifted from a flight through time to an object occupying space. It remains to be seen whether the vitality and authority of the ancient oral tales will translate well into written literature.

There is some evidence already to suggest that they will, at least in modified form. Some contemporary authors, born into an oral culture, have found a voice and an audience in print. *The Woman Warrior* by Maxine Hong Kingston (1977) is a vivid tale specifically about the conflict suffered by a person caught between the discourses of two different cultures, one oral and one literate. It is an autobiographical account written by a woman born into a Chinese peasant family recently immigrated to California. Steeped through early childhood in the myths and stories of her mother's culture half a world away, Kingston was then thrust into an ordinary American public school, where—confronted with the denial of all those narratives by which she had defined herself—she felt herself to be invisible and mute. This book is the story of how, embracing both traditions, she discovered her voice.

A book like *The Woman Warrior* expands the boundaries of literature and shrinks the distance between peoples. Other writers from mixed backgrounds are capturing the imagination of readers. Amy Tan, also Chinese American, writes of the love and conflict between Chinese mothers and their Americanized daughters. Leslie Marmon Silko, a Native American, transcribes the mythic stories she grew up with and tells others about the chasms that separate modern Indians from both their own heritage and the larger American culture. Gabriel García Márquez writes as product and observer of an exuberantly sprawling Latin American peasant culture. These writers and many others are bringing some of the authority of the storyteller back into English-American literary tradition.

There is another audience discovering the appeal of tales from oral and folk cultures, an audience for whom the enchantment of story has never diminished: young children. When I asked my son recently what he was reading to Nick, my six-year-old grandson, he showed me three books they had just chosen together from the shelves of the local library. One was a Blackfoot Indian legend, one a Japanese fable about a rabbit, one a traditional Chinese tale about dragons. A subsequent visit to the children's shelves proved that this cultural variety was no coincidence. Beatrix Potter and Dr. Seuss are keeping company with a whole rainbow of traditional storytellers. Here is a cheering turn of events: while scholars are wrangling over the literate-white-male supremacy of the literary canon from above, it is being subverted by an influx of other cultures from below. Perhaps by the time Nick is in high school, the literary works of oral and minority cultures will be as accessible to him as Ernest Hemingway is to my students now, and he will hear truth from many tongues.

Practical Matters

The ordinary conversational narratives of adolescents are full of delicious detail. I hear vivid snatches as they come into the room before class, talking intensely in pairs or small groups. Unfortunately, adolescents who are put into the more formal situation of telling a story to the class tend to stiffen up and distance themselves from the event, leaving out just those crucial little details that keep the memory alive and ought to give life to the telling of it.

I like to plan a personal storytelling session after a unit of reading and writing poetry with an emphasis on sensory language. We read small poems by such poets as Amy Lowell, Emily Dickinson, William Carlos Williams, Carl Sandburg — poets whose images become reality on the page. I bring in interesting objects for students to look at, handle, sniff, and evoke in words. We close our eyes, listen to nothing for a few minutes, and then write.

When the class is keenly aware of sensory stimuli, I ask them to recall an apparently insignificant event in their lives that nevertheless made some impact on them. They visualize the event, then brainstorm and jot down all the sensory details they can remember surrounding it. Often students make for themselves the discovery that the event was memorable because it was a highly stimulating sensory experience.

I model the exercise by telling them (for example) of a time I went walking on the Maine coast in winter and got stranded on a spit of sand by the incoming tide. I brainstorm aloud the sensations I remember: "The wind billowed my jacket and pushed so hard I had to lean into it; I could smell the salt of the sea; the sand was wet, very cold, and unyielding under my feet; I heard gulls crying and waves crashing and hissing on the shore.... "

The final step is to rehearse telling the story, using the sensory details to make it alive and real to the listener. Students may rehearse at school with a partner, or at home with a parent or a mirror or the dog, before telling their stories to the class the next day.

This exercise is valuable for several reasons. The stories are not only colorful in detail, but unusual; the effort to resurrect an apparently insignificant event yields surprises for both tellers and listeners. It also connects poetry to narrative, using the skills of one discipline to enhance another.

≡*Five*

Reenactment

*T*he students in my Shakespeare class were having a difficult time conceptualizing the conflict between Prince Hal and his father in the third act of *King Henry IV* Part 1. Why was Hal so rebellious? Why, on the other hand, did he choose at that moment to respect his father's wishes? If Henry was so fed up with Hal, why did he send for him? What did he want or expect from him? "We'd better act it out," the class agreed (in this heterogeneously grouped junior/senior class, "act it out" meant improvise).

Matthew volunteered to play Prince Hal, Adam to play King Henry. The directors, their classmates, began with Matthew. The words here are taken from my hasty transcript and are not complete, but they catch the spirit of the comments.

"Now, you've come back to help him, but he doesn't know that yet." "He's mad at you. You've been *bad*. So you know he's gonna chew you out." "It's not like you feel guilty." "No, you're not too hassled about it. You're like, 'Yeah, Dad, okay, I'll just wait while you blow your cool.'"

Matthew lounged against a desk, looked at his fingernails, nonchalant. "Like this?"

"That's good." The class then turned its attention to Adam. A tall, straight figure, he stood with his back to Matthew and listened impassively to his classmates as they told him, "You're really mad at this kid. Actually you're furious." "Hanging out with thieves." "You've got a war to fight and where is he?" "You're like so ashamed of him, you wish he wasn't even your kid. You wish Hotspur was your kid instead."

I waited through the ritual small silence to make sure there were no more comments, then said to Matthew and Adam, "Are you ready? Go."

Instantly Adam whirled on Matthew, his posture all aggression. Hands clenched into fists at his sides, face distorted and red, tendons standing out like ropes on his arms and neck, he cried, "HOW CAN YOU CALL YOURSELF *MY SON!*"

Matthew fell back over the desk with a clatter. His eyes and mouth flew open wide from shock. Then he and all his classmates laughed, but with the laughter came the "Oh!" of comprehension. "*That's* how it was!"

Improvisation: Learning Through Play

When students "act out" a scene from literature—not just drama; the same principles apply to any story—they start with the words on the page as their only clues. From those words, they work in two directions: inward, to find the feelings and motivations that prompt the character to speak the words, and outward, leading to the action that results from them.[1] Shakespeare's plays are singularly open to this sort of interpretation, partly because they are great literature posing timeless questions, partly because virtually all the reader gets is dialogue. Shakespeare passed on to us little in the way of setting and stage directions, but much in terms of human interaction. The daunting difficulty of his language becomes a peripheral problem when feelings on one side and action on the other emerge to clarify what he is saying.

Improvisation is especially appealing to many students because it involves play. Teenagers still keenly recall participating in the constant reenactments of childhood: "Let's play house," "Let's play monsters." It is not such a great or threatening step from there to "Let's play Shakespeare." Improvisation, a collaborative activity, allows students momentarily to lay aside the need "to keep their social and academic lives apart by internalizing the

---

[1] I am indebted to Alan (Mokler) MacVey, who introduced me to a more complete and artistic form of this technique for exploring a dramatic text.

49

radical separation of work and play that traditional forms of education demand" (Trimbur 1985, 90).

Learning by Living the Experience

Improvisation is only one approach (albeit a very good one) to reenactment. Reenactment is any activity that converts the written or verbal record of experience back into the realm of actual experience. It is one of the most powerful learning devices a teacher can invoke, because by re-creating and participating in an experience, students incorporate it into their certain knowledge of the world. Chemistry teachers have known this for a long time. Their students continually repeat and verify for themselves the basic experiments on which the field has built for decades. Small wonder Anglo-American culture tends to regard scientific data as a more valid truth than literary art. Its reproduction is a mechanical process, easily assessed for accuracy, and not dependent upon the affect of the learner.

Our literate culture is far removed from any oral tradition that revitalizes its stories from one generation to the next. It is too easy for students and teachers alike to see the culture's stories as belonging to unnamed others, far removed from our daily lives and probably long dead. It takes effort on the part of both teacher and student to reach the point, movingly described by a high school girl in Robert Coles' *The Call of Stories*, where "the story becomes yours. No, I don't mean 'your story'; I mean you have imagined what those people look like, and how they speak the words in the book, and how they move around, and so you and the writer are in cahoots" (1989, 64).

Actively Engaging the Text

To re-create a chemistry experiment requires data, materials, and equipment; to re-create a narrative requires nothing more than imagination. To meet such a seemingly simple requirement, how can a teacher best bring an author and a teenager into "cahoots"? The answer is as various as the kids in her class. A teacher may encourage her students to summarize or paraphrase; to keep a journal or a learning log; to create an individual-effort picture or a group-effort bulletin board; to view a film or listen to the words of a respected elder; to sculpt, sew, sing, draw, or paint; to discuss, research, or argue; to improvise or act. In any case, it is the students themselves who are doing something to breathe life into the story. A teacher can clear paths and set up signposts, but she can't transplant the marvelous resonances of a great story straight from her head to theirs.

It's too easy to think of English class as primarily passive, a course where students sit quietly letting the words of the teacher and the text flow into their blank spaces. The language of such a classroom is imposed from the outside and remains, to some degree, alien to those for whom it is intended. Students who actively engage the text, however, develop a dialogue with the author and with each other. Their language is alive and flexible; it embraces the discourses of multiple cultures (including that of the author) and brings them into communication. In a very real sense, any effective classroom becomes a unique mini-culture with its own history, folklore, and language genre.

What Happened? The Role of Summary

The most basic uses of language are among the most important to learning; sadly, they are often discouraged by teachers who are focused on the achievement of a higher order of cognition. Teachers may ask their students to skip over the very steps that will eventually lead to the sort of sophisticated response they seek. But when students are meeting the narrative of an author from another century or a cultural setting radically different from their own, they need to be able to start with the apparently simplest of questions: "What happened?" Often, adolescents who have conscientiously read the assignment just don't have the life experience to make sense of the event it presents, and this is true not only of literature but of the content areas as well. Here is where a plain old-fashioned summary, written in a learning log or spoken in a small group setting, can be very helpful. It's hard to "go deeper" into the subtleties of a text until the action itself is clear.

There are certain passages that cry out for summary. Generally they are complex stories in which some of the cultural expectations of the characters are unfamiliar to modern readers. The encounter between Odysseus and the Cyclops is one of these. Ancient Greek ideas of social obligation and hospitality underlie the intense conflicts in this episode, and students often have trouble figuring out *what* happens because it's not clear to them *why* it happens or what might result. Summarizing the action leads them naturally to ask *what* and *why*. Odysseus confronts Polyphemus: why? The Cyclops brutalizes his men: why? Odysseus blinds the Cyclops: why? Polyphemus prays to Poseidon for revenge: what's going to happen? In retelling the events of the narrative, students conjecture about their causes and possible outcomes, raising some profound questions and leading to the kind of analytical thinking that expands knowledge and eventually results in good writing.

Bringing the Story into the Present: Paraphrasing

To create an accurate summary forces the reader to go back and interact with the text and begins the process of re-creating the experience. Another good way to clarify a difficult passage is to paraphrase it. It is in paraphrasing, in using words to resituate an event from some distant time or place into the context of their own, that students summon up the liveliest language. I am often impressed by the variety of speech genres available to modern young Americans. When improvising, my students usually speak much as they do among themselves, without varnish; but when writing a paraphrase, they may opt for a totally different style, most likely one that reinforces the artistic intentions of the author they are paraphrasing. Here, for example, a high school senior from a white rural community translates a bit of Shakespeare into a popular teen subcultural language that draws heavily upon black urban speech. In the original passage from *A Midsummer Night's Dream*, Helena envies Hermia's beauty and success in love:

HERMIA: God speed fair Helena! Whither away?
HELENA: Call you me fair? That fair again unsay.
Demetrius loves your fair. O happy fair!

Your eyes are lodestars, and your tongue's sweet air
More tunable than lark to shepherd's ear,
When wheat is green, when hawthorn buds appear.
Sickness is catching. O, were favor so,
Yours would I catch, fair Hermia, ere I go;
My ear should catch your voice, my eye your eye,
My tongue should catch your tongue's sweet melody.
Were the world mine, Demetrius being bated,
The rest I'd give to be to you translated.
O, teach me how you look, and with what art
You sway the motion of Demetrius' heart!

HERMIA: I frown upon him, yet he loves me still.
HELENA: O that your frowns would teach my smiles such skill!
HERMIA: I give him curses, yet he gives me love.
HELENA: O that my prayers could such affection move!
HERMIA: The more I hate, the more he follows me.
HELENA: The more I love, the more he hateth me.
HERMIA: His folly, Helena, is no fault of mine.
HELENA: None, but your beauty: would that fault were mine!
HERMIA: Take comfort. He no more shall see my face;
Lysander and myself will fly this place.
Before the time I did Lysander see,
Seemed Athens as a paradise to me.
O, then, what graces in my love do dwell,
That he hath turned a heaven unto a hell!

(I, i, 180–207)

Tiffany's version turns inside out the humor of the girls' courtly speech: Shakespeare's is funny because it's so formal, Tiffany's because it's so blatantly *in*formal. What Tiffany has understood (at the artistic if not the critical level) and adopted for her paraphrase is the fact that the two girls are chained to the language of a particular social stratum. She chooses a social identity somewhere near the other end of the spectrum, to amusing effect:

HERMIA: Girlfriend, where you goin'? You are so hot!
HELENA: Me hot?! No, no, no honey chi'. Demetrius say you hot!
Your eyes shine like bi ol' diamonds! You talk so fine! Your
words are cooler than Down-Town Julie Brown's. It would be

like so totally wild to be like you. If I knew all you cool words, like fur sure Demetrius would be all over me. —Show me how! Tell your words and where you shop and who on earth does that crazy hair of yours? Demetrius loves all that kind o' stuff.

HERMIA: Honey, you can have him. I yell and slap and the geek keeps runnin' fur more!

HELENA: What words did you yell at him?

HERMIA: I treat him like total shit Helena, but the boy won't take a hint.

HELENA: He'd like not be too cool with me if I did that.

HERMIA: I ignore the fool, but he follows me like a pathetic dog!

HELENA: I'm trying real hard to make him like me but he just gives me these really bogus looks.

HERMIA: Well babe, it's not my fault he's so screwed up.

HELENA: Please! You are drop-dead gorgeous. I wish I had such problems.

HERMIA: Yo baby yo! Open your ears! He won't be looking at me no more anyhow. Lysander and I see we like dissin' this place. No more, no how, no way.

—TIFFANY, 16

Tiffany is boldly different, but still true to the original spirit in her re-creation of this dramatic dialogue. She respects the importance of style in the way Shakespeare says things and therefore chooses a contemporary style appropriate to the content of the particular scene in which to fashion her response. Her bit of work goes well beyond simple paraphrase. It is a creative adaptation that falls somewhere between enactment, the invention of an original utterance, and *re*-enactment, the imaginative conversion of another's words into the experience they describe. Without doubt, she has a firm grasp on the important elements of this scene: the conflicts, the unawakened and undifferentiated character of the two girls as well as their genuine friendship, and their need to reject a safely familiar, civilized setting to find out who they really are. Tiffany intuits and effectively exploits the concept that the social speech of teenagers is less an effective form of communication than a cover for what they don't know.

Reenactment as a Conduit for Creativity

When adolescents embark on endeavors of reenactment, the teacher needs to be receptive and flexible, because this is the moment when he yields control of the educational experience. He may always be sure that someone will come winging in with a surprise. Most students write, act, or draw something conventional and directly related to the work under study, and they do learn from the process; but some, like Tiffany, catch a spark and carry the assignment to an inspired level. Here is where the culture of the classroom takes on the richness of shared experience, and everyone in it, including the teacher, makes an unexpected cognitive leap.

A few years ago, for example, I asked a group of about sixty freshmen to bring to life some aspect of *Huckleberry Finn*. Fifty-six turned the whole back wall of the classroom into the Mississippi River with episodes illustrated along its length, created and presented skits, or researched and shared all kinds of material about Mark Twain, slavery, western expansion, literary irony, and so on. Four presented a scene from the Wilks episode as comic opera. (In this episode, the duke and the dolphin, two scalawags who have joined Huck and Jim in their journey down the Mississippi, pose as the brothers of the newly deceased Peter Wilks in order to claim the inheritance that should rightly go to Peter's nieces.)

I was severe with these four students: "You may do this only if you sing good and loud and with a straight face." Their main problem was finding a place to rehearse—they got kicked out of every area of the school. But their scene, belted out at top volume, with the exaggerated gestures of *opéra bouffe*, captured Twain's satiric force as none of the more conventional projects could. The students' interpretation made clear the villainous greed of the duke and dolphin, Mary Jane Wilks's beguiling innocence and generosity, and the music-hall absurdity of the situation that had brought them together.

In the process of developing their opera from a complex, difficult narrative passage, these freshmen went far beyond a simple understanding of "What happened?" But that's where they started. They soon discovered that the episode implied much more than a simple series of events. When they explored their characters, turning inward to find the motivations and outward to see the resulting actions, everything they said and did seemed skewed from reality. Taking a clue from the ridiculous gestures of the "deaf and dumb" duke and another from the well-timed appearance of the noble Dr. Robinson, they began to perceive that a grotesque interpretation fitted the scene much better than any attempt to play it straight. And they helped fifty-six other freshmen to share the savage funniness of Twain's vision better than anything this teacher could have done.

Reenactment as Process

Obviously not every harebrained-sounding idea for reenactment comes out this well. Projects don't get finished, or the members of a group don't agree at some level, or students fail to communicate successfully whatever it is they have discovered. But the whole point of reenactment is to go through a *process*, to *experience* in some form the event and the meaning of an event. This process is therefore potentially much more important than any product that might result—even though it is easier to assess a product than the partly invisible, partly subjective journey a student took in its creation.

It is in reenactment, specifically, that students most need room to fail without fear of judgment, for it is here that they take control of their own learning. The teacher who is receptive to student initiatives needs also to be generous with the results: to credit the intent. Students who are engaged and trying, even if they fumble along the way, are more likely to succeed in the end—even on those objective assessments that assume a certain distance from the required task.

Most teachers develop over the years a mental library of magic moments that sustain them in the classroom. The majority of mine come from those scary, exciting times when, after doing whatever seemed essential to bring students and literature together, I have relinquished control and sat back to watch what happened:

- Jack, a deer hunter in real life, clambered up onto a desk and changed from a silent, retiring, round-shouldered youngster to a terrifying Odysseus towering above the suitors, his features intent and merciless, bow arched for the kill.
- Richard mustered his rock band in the cafeteria to play an original song for his American Lit class, which had just finished reading *The Scarlet Letter*. Prancing in front of the drummer and bass player, flapping his guitar like a wing, he sang: "Baby Pearl, Baby Pearl, She was her Daddy's little girl . . . "
- Notoriously macho Paul, thirty minutes into a discussion of prejudice inspired by the trial in *To Kill a Mockingbird*, said, "It was just color back then, but now it's sex too. Guys in our society give women a hard time for no reason. Women ought to have the same chance as men." There were long moments of awed, breathless silence, and then Karen, who was always on Paul's case, said, *"Thank you!"*

PEANUTS reprinted by permission of UFS, Inc.

These students, by bringing their reading to life and sharing the immediate reality of written words with their classmates, wedded the abstract world of academic learning to the practical world of experience. At some level, they not only comprehended the reading passage, but also lived the event, which connected with and became important to their own understanding of the world. Their participation in the event became part of the shared culture of the classroom. Listening and reading are not abstract exercises, even though the components of response to the content may be abstracted. Chief among the cognitive strategies that contribute to reading comprehension are predicting, generating questions, summarizing and clarifying (Cazden 1988, 8). Reenactment in its various forms encompasses all these strategies while giving both teacher and student a wide scope in choice of means. It also gives the teacher a valid arena from which to bow out while leaving the work—and the excitement of discovery—up to the students.

Practical Matters

Reenactment involves performance—and stage fright. Like actors in a play, students who take the risk to live the experience of a story do so symbolically, converting an event that has been represented in language into a new event that includes their own interpretation. It's obvious that I encourage performance in my classroom practice. A genre that lends itself particularly well to interpretation in performance is the ballad. Early in the year, I like to model narrative intensity and risk-taking behavior by singing ballads in class.

Adolescents are familiar with ballads, of course—not the ones that I sing, but no matter; the themes never change. The words that flow into my students through their little black foam earplugs are still about love, betrayal, adventure, and death. Most teenagers have strong emotional attachments to a number of current songs. On tapes or disks, they bring their ballads to share, and I sing mine. To sing in public is a heavy risk for me; my small voice does well to maintain a melody. But I plunge in and try to invest the words with a commitment and feeling worthy of the splendid old ballads.

After I've broken the dangerous ice, some of the students will also sing. I'm always surprised by the ones who do, just as they were surprised by me. Song, like story, reaches across cultural and generational boundaries to make unexpected connections. Once the school's top athlete visited my ninth-grade classes to sing "Lord Randall" with me, doing more as he perished at my feet to break down the school's "jock" stereotype than a year's worth of affective education units.

Traditional ballads are a wonderful medium for introducing a number of linguistic concepts because the genre is already so familiar. Furthermore, although rich in feeling and strict in structure, ballads are not difficult in content. The challenge of the traditional ballads lies in their unfamiliar language. Much more readily than in the works of Shakespeare or Chaucer, teenagers faced with differing versions of "Lord Randall" or "The Twa Corbies" pick up both the forms and vocabulary of old English. They also are intrigued by the evidence that words, phrases, and whole lyrics modify over time and across cultures.

☰ Six

Culture, Genre, and the Adolescent Writer

I was one of a group of American tourists standing around a small elaborately carved stele amidst the majestic ruins of Tulum. Our tour guide, a Mayan Indian named Miguel, was on his knees in the middle of the group, eagerly drawing with a pebble in the earth as he explained the ancient Mayan mathematical system carved in the stone. I looked at the people around me, comfortable middle-aged Americans, all craning their necks, listening, and staring with intense absorption at the difficult concepts taking shape in the dust. Miguel was a born teacher. Proud of his culture, steeped in its stories, he had spent the day bringing our group to such a state of need for his knowledge that there we stood under the hot Mexican sun, oblivious for the moment to the glorious ruins and to the less fortunate sightseers milling around us, completely entranced by a complex lesson in math. I still remember how to compute in Mayan.

The Difficulties of Teaching in a Multicultural Democracy

All teachers hope to achieve what Miguel was achieving so successfully. They hope to take some portion of their culture that they particularly value and share it, keep it vital, by arousing and satisfying a need for it in those they teach. By the nature of their work, teachers are conservators. They accept, often uneasily, the constraints of acting within a social institution established by the common culture for the purposes of perpetuating that culture. The uneasiness comes from a more or less conscious awareness that, in a democracy, education has the paradoxical duty not only to inculcate a set of social and cultural values but also to empower the students to question, interact with, and change those values. Furthermore, teachers are continuously aware that their students bring diverse cultural expectations from their homes to the classroom. If the system is working effectively, social change feeds into, emanates from, threatens, and enriches the educational establishment in a constant cycle.

The concept of "common culture" in the United States is more myth than reality. Because of its size and its polyglot social history, the U.S. has always assumed that its schools would deal, effectively or not, with a regional as well as a national culture. Up to the present day, American schools and communities have coped with waves of immigrants by absorbing them. In general, the immigrants have been willing to be absorbed; they came to America because it looked like a better place to them, for whatever reason, than their own home.

The first-generation children of immigrants undergo a profound cultural disorientation, because the language and values in which they are steeped at home are so different from those they learn at school. Maxine Hong Kingston's autobiography, *The Woman Warrior* (see chapter 4), tells the moving story of a Chinese-American girl's struggle to reconcile the conflicting cultures of her childhood; surely it is a story that has been told a million times over in scores of languages and dialects. But Kingston makes clear the resolution of her conflict: she calls herself a Chinese *American*, and it is within the American cultural framework that she has made a successful life. Up to this point in U.S. history the immigrants and their children have generally chosen to accommodate themselves without significant protest to their new social setting.

The exceptions, of course, were the Africans, who did not come by choice. The growing awareness by African Americans of their minority group status, and their increasingly visible protest against an oppression that has deep social and historical roots, has given birth since the sixties to a new attitude among American minorities. Instead of disappearing into the mainstream or struggling along cultural byways, immigrants and women and gays and Native Americans and all sorts of other subgroups now want the American society as a whole to expand its cultural definitions (and certainly its economic opportunities also) to include them. This movement has raised fundamental questions about the structure and purpose of all American institutions, none more than the school. If it is the task of schools to educate the young in the body of knowledge of a common culture, how are all these newly self-assertive groups to be accommodated? How much responsibility should the school assume for accommodating them, considering the fact that historically it has been they who accommodated to the schools? What kind of curriculum will sustain the social fabric and at the same time meet this tremendous array of needs?

The Discontinuity Between English Language, British Curriculum, and American Culture

Ideally, the stories of all those diverse peoples who have converged to form our pluralistic democratic society would be woven into its social fabric. The public institutions of such a society, including its schools, would affirm the histories and values of all citizens, at the same time offering all of them the equal opportunity to partake of a common social and cultural experience. Cultures are not driven by ideals, however, even though governments may be: the design of our democracy was forged by idealistic men, but cultures are always in process, continually evolving and developing their traditions. Therefore, old, current, and emergent ideas, often contradictory, exist side by side in the same social setting. American public schools have trouble weaving into their curricula the narratives of a diverse population because those schools were established upon and still embody a contradiction between old and new ideas.

Universal public education came into being as one of the more idealistic structures of the new American society, but a new curriculum was not part of the package. Because England was the dominant force in the colonies, and English the dominant language, the British curriculum was the model for our

PEANUTS reprinted by permission of UFS, Inc.

early schools and to a great extent remains so today. The name of the school subject that centers in the common language of the culture is not "American," but "English" (and the departments that call it Language Arts are begging the issue). Thus the egalitarian schools of this large multicultural young country presented its children with an elitist educational model borrowed from a homogeneous, insular, and ancient society.

For a long time the notion of "culture" as a privileged body of knowledge was held separate from the everyday world of work and social interchange. The range of available knowledge wasn't so wide then; to know "the canon" was to be educated, and to be educated was to possess power—in America, literally to be enfranchised. (Even as recently as the 1920s, the president of Harvard University, Charles W. Eliot, claimed that all a man needed to be truly educated could fit on a five-foot shelf; challenged, he produced the Harvard Classics.)

In this century, the canon has taken on a mythic quality. As the sciences have split off into separate disciplines, the definition of *canon* has been both narrowed to mean only literature and broadened to include new works that have met some arbitrary test of critical acclaim. It has been cherished, both here and in England, by those who believe it represents in our culture the constant standard for art, truth, and morality; it has been denigrated by those who feel it is no longer relevant to an industrialized, scientific, rapidly changing world. It has been elbowed aside, particularly in the U.S., by a popular culture that combines the bold and vigorous with the commercial and exploitative. And where do we find the canon today? It rests on the shelves of America's English departments, in various stages of use and disuse, a joy and a puzzle to the teachers who love great literature and love kids, for whom that literature may often seem inappropriate.

The English Curriculum in a Multicultural Society

Any discussion of curriculum and canon returns to the question: just what is it that today's American adolescents *should* be learning? Of what does the subject *English* consist? It is not—like history or science—a discrete body of knowledge, a collection of data with its own discourse and logic. Thus the canon does not define English, because it is selected by value judgment rather than by the internal coherence of its elements. Nor is English, like Spanish or Japanese, a study of language as a communication system. In studying a foreign language we are dependent upon linguists and lexicographers, those encoders who provide the semantic rules and meanings that allow us entry; but in English these structures are already in place when we start school, as are the cultural mores embedded within them. The point is to *use* the language as a tool within the grasp to open up other areas of learning. Tony Burgess gives the best definition I've read when he says, "Language [i.e., English] is an arena rather than a subject and has always been multidisciplinary" (1988, 155), and he suggests as a corollary that a common vision of English teaching, an agreement on what the adolescent *ought* to learn, may not be altogether desirable in a multicultural society: "Consensus, a common approach, may finish by excluding or trimming divergent or critical opinions. What may be needed, rather, is openness to different views" (155).

If there is disagreement on what students ought to *learn* through studying English, there is greater concord about what they ought to learn how to *do*: read, write, and speak effectively. This just circles right back to the original question, though: English teachers have to tread a fine line between the demands of curriculum and the apparent needs of their students in deciding *what* should be read, written, and said. By what criteria is the literature to be chosen? How are the students to appreciate the literature they read or hear and make it their own? What sorts of accommodation should be made for students whose English is nonstandard or a second language, and for students whose social background differs from that of the common culture?

The Role of Genre in the English Class

At the intersection of these various issues — the canon, the "subject" of English, cultural diversity in the classroom, and philosophical diversity in approaches to teaching English — I want to introduce the concept of genre. The word *genre*, originally used to denote a literary form, has become a catch-all term for any type of popular formula fiction such as mystery, romance, western, and so on. I would like to consider these two uses of the word (including formula TV shows as well as written fiction), plus a further connotation: genre as a reflector of the culture that produces it. I would like further to contend that writing narrative within the framework of any genre can be an excellent learning experience for adolescents. The rigid formal rules of popular genre may appear to constrain narrative creativity, but paradoxically, by providing a ready-made structure, they free young writers to explore more sensitive issues of identity, values, and meanings.

As Gemma Moss points out in *Un/Popular Fictions*, genre writing for an older child fills very much the same role as fantasy play for a younger child. Both activities are dependent upon culturally established rules to structure the freely imagined events. She mentions Vygotsky's concept that "action in play is subordinated to the meaning of things," and asserts that "by deploying a particular genre and watching what it throws into relief young writers are speculating about the future and working out how it could be understood in terms of what they already know. They are playing with meaning" (1989, 114).

Moss, a teacher in a British high school, does a close reading of several romances written by her adolescent students and defines very clearly their search for meaning and value within a conventional form. Unfortunately, in American high schools, little fiction writing (especially with free choice of subject and form) is encouraged at all. By the time our students reach high school, any fiction they may be producing is usually written on their own time to meet a private need. It is mostly in the elementary and middle years that American teachers have a chance to see and use the powerful organizing role of popular genre in a student's written work. I believe, however, that genre writing is one of the forms of storytelling that can contribute a great deal to adolescents' self-knowledge and understanding of their own and other cultures.

Moss restricts her exploration of student genre writing to the romance, and I gather that this is a compelling form for a large percentage of English teenage girls. I've found American students to be more eclectic. The long historic multicultural diversity of the United States has given rise to a great smorgasbord of popular genres from which students may pick and choose those that best fit their needs; they learn by trying on different forms as well as by playing with different meanings. By the time students reach high school, many have begun to combine or experiment with forms. Echoes of a variety of genres appear in the narratives of my students. Romances and social problem stories are popular with the girls; adventure, mystery, and horror attract the boys. The most common genre employed by the adolescents I teach is the adventure fantasy. The form is not gender specific, although issues of gender emerge depending on the model and the student author; boys write in response to such authors as J.R.R. Tolkien and Piers Antony, girls in response to writers like Robin McKinley and Anne McCaffrey.

Model Genres

"Dungeons and Dragons" I first became aware of genre as a living force in the classroom (rather than as a scrap of literary vocabulary to be defined on a test) a number of years ago when several of my junior high students began turning in long, complex stories based on the "Dungeons and Dragons" game. Like all popular genres, this game tells stories that are tightly structured, predictable, and rigidly adherent to a particular moral stance; but it has an especially compelling narrative drive because the player actually *becomes* the knight, wizard, or whatever character he chooses and by his own actions creates the story within a given framework. The students writing these stories were boys, fascinated by computers, good students in a school where scholarship is not considered a masculine quality — in other words, they formed a distinct cultural minority of a sort found in *any* school, not just those of mixed race or national origin. "Dungeons and Dragons" offered these boys a formal context within which to explore issues of vital interest to them: gender identity, friendship and conflict, the role of intelligence in heroism, the fearful struggle between good and evil in the world.

Having connected "Dungeons and Dragons" in my mind to "social subset of scholarly boys," I began to conceive of genre as having not just a literary but a cultural significance. People (not only young ones; many adults love mysteries, Gothic romances, spy thrillers) read popular genre fiction for pleasure. The pleasure must derive from the working out of a fantasy within a strict form, since form and fantasy are the only common elements of all genre fiction. The fantasies, which are individual visions, give shape to our dreams of what *might be*; the forms, which are a cultural product, provide rules to establish the way things *must be*. Ultimately all literature works in this way: the more artistic the work, the more subtle the interplay of content and structure. The young reader and writer chooses his genre according to societal issues that are important to him; he is free to follow his fantasies no matter what unique direction they may take, because in adhering to form they follow some accepted set of cultural rules.

"The Hunt"   We all identify ourselves culturally by the stories we tell and the rules we follow. Thus cultural groups find or create their own genres to define and validate themselves. A member of a cultural minority, like Maxine Hong Kingston, may take a genre from the literary mainstream, such as autobi-ography, and manipulate the form to meet her own needs for identity. Students in the rural Vermont school where I teach have a genre of their own, modeled not on any popular genre I'm aware of but on the activities and legends of their own com-munity: this is the story of The Hunt. The form is strict: a sol-itary hunter penetrates and attunes himself to a natural setting in which he meets and eventually kills a wild animal. The story defines the worth and manhood of each boy who writes it. Even the most taciturn Vermont hill dweller, like Shawn, who wrote seldom and spoke almost never, has a powerful voice—in which echo the voices of his forebears and neighbors—for describing The Hunt:

> All alone in this big space of nothingness—but it wasnt nothingness, trees all over, the smell of pine in the air. But not a sound past my ear except the fresh snow hitting the ground benethe me. And the crunch of snow as I crushed it with my boots as I was following the trail of a massive bear, its tracks were as big as my feet. His trail was slowly disapearing.
>
> But then as I lost his trail a thundering crash came from behind me. And as I turned around to look I saw the biggest beast in my life. He stood as tall as a tree. He gave out the feercest call of ter-ror that seemed to echoe on forever.

Then I saw him draw closer. I felt the cold medal of my gun run across my hand as I pulled it up to aim. Then the smell of smoke filled the air as I skweezed six shells of fire into the beast, dropping it in a mighty crash of death.

—Shawn, 15

Teachers' Suspicions of Popular Genres

In general, teachers dislike or at best tolerate student narratives based on popular genres. There are good historic reasons for this in the way they have been brought up and trained to value literature. These stories are unoriginal, stereotypical, derivative, *boring.* A friend who teaches sixth grade tossed a fistful of papers onto the faculty room couch and sighed, "I'm so tired of car chases and gun fights!" She leafed through the papers, rejected a retelling of last night's TV adventures in Hawaii, then paused, read, and handed over for my shared approval a retelling of last night's family adventures at the Burlington Square Mall. In each case the student was trying faithfully to re-create events held in memory, seeking meaning in them by naming, ordering, prioritizing. The first story was structured by TV adventure formula, the second by home and classroom conventions. The second paper was more pleasing—I must agree—to the cultural expectations of teachers, but the value of the first paper in terms of student learning was probably as great. Any piece of writing derives its structure from some cultural model; it is the search for meaning within the chosen model that is significant for the learner.

Teachers dislike popular genre fiction for other more serious reasons, however. Besides being unoriginal, the models of genre—books and magazines off the newsstand, TV drama, comedy, and cartoons—are seen to be both morally suspect (full of violence, sexual innuendo, and stereotypical language) and so inferior to the literature offered in school as to be destructive to the development of literary appreciation. Because these stories are accessible and young people read or watch them for pleasure, teachers fear that they will swallow the values whole; in Moss's words:

Great power is attributed to pleasure, a power greater than force, yet it is curiously seen as working in the same way: to control and subdue. Moreover, those who succumb to pleasure are seen to be doing so mindlessly. They surrender themselves to it. It acts upon them. How does this square with educational theories of reading which acknowledge that readers must actively involve themselves in constructing meaning from the text? (1989, 42)

Moss goes on to demonstrate convincingly that it is precisely the values of popular fiction with which student writers engage; they use the forms as an arena in which to grapple with issues.

It's a cliché that Americans live in a violent, divided society. Popular genre fiction, in all its raw sensationalism, diversity, and wide availability, comes much closer to defining a common culture for Americans than does the English canon. Indeed, seen in this light, "the canon" might even be considered the chosen genre of a social subset called English teachers. It has its place, and a central place, certainly, in the English class; but it is only one specialized part of the world of literature and story that we have the option of making available to our students. The Renaissance English of Shakespeare is stranger to my rural New England-born students than the black speech rhythms of Toni Morrison or the tough slick urban language of detective fiction (and any teacher who objects to violence, sex, and death in literature had better not teach *Romeo and Juliet*). It is a paradoxical truth that to participate in the common culture of America is to become conversant with the dialects and often conflicting conventions of the diverse cultures of which it is composed.

The Language of Minority Cultures

Some subcultures remain too far removed to partake of the common culture. The unresolved questions about how to teach minority students, those who are economically deprived and who speak nonstandard English, are not so much educational as basic social issues. Labov convincingly contests the educational establishment's well-intentioned misperception that these children are verbally deprived, and can be remediated; their language is not inferior, just different:

The essential fallacy of the verbal deprivation theory lies in tracing the educational failure of the child to his personal deficiencies. At present, these deficiencies are said to be caused by the home environment. It is traditional to explain a child's failure in school by his inadequacy; but when failure reaches such massive proportions, it seems to us necessary to look at the social and cultural obstacles to learning, and the inability of the school to adjust to the social situation. (1972, 208)

In many cases these children learn their values within a cultural subgroup that is not only outside of but alienated from the common culture. Do we have the right to try to persuade and educate young people to be successful in a society they reject? If, as English teachers, we accept and validate students' nonstandard English dialect, are we setting them up for subsequent failure in an economic system run on standard English? Is it our responsibility to give them words with which to rail against their fate? If the school is unable to adjust to the social situation, good argument can be made that it is the social situation itself that needs adjusting. It is a great deal to ask of a school to mediate between a dominant culture and an alienated subculture.

Interestingly, Operation Head Start, a program for which Labov predicted failure because it was "designed to repair the child, rather than the school" (1972, 208) has proven successful: "Head Start graduates have been found to have better attendance, miss fewer tests, need special education less and drop out less often" (Cooper 1990). But the reasons cited for this success have nothing to do with "repairing the child." Minimally funded, Operation Head Start from its inception had to depend upon the participation of the local community in running the program; it actively involved the families, especially the mothers, of the children. In other words, it did mediate between the dominant culture and the alienated subculture and brought these families back from hopelessness and rejection to a renewed vision of the American dream. One program coordinator actually described Head Start as "a parent involvement program that happens to serve children" (Worthen 1992). Cooper suggests that the grassroots structuring of Operation Head Start may serve as a model for helping public schools adjust to the social situation.

Embracing All Cultures and Genres in the English Class

Teachers in the setting of an alienated subculture have a much more difficult job than those in a mainstream school. Their techniques will be different, but at the individual classroom level the goals are the same: to provide, however possible, the arena in which students may learn to read, write, and speak effectively. I think of the Mayan tour guide, Miguel, who with stories and enthusiasm beguiled his class of Americans into the position of *wanting* to understand Mayan mathematics. English teachers have all kinds of stories at their disposal, and presumably they are enthusiastic about them. They are in a unique position, first, to validate the experience of students by introducing them to genres and literature written from their own social background. My Vermont students enjoy and deeply understand the stories of Howard Frank Mosher and the poetry of Robert Frost, for example. Also teachers can tap into the popular genres of the wider common culture and support the uses their students make of them. And, like Miguel, English teachers are in a unique position to open out new cultural horizons by sharing stories of other times and places.

All literature, *all* kinds of stories, are viable models for the narratives written by adolescents, no matter what their cultural background. The more narratives they are exposed to, the more they can fit into their world picture, the better. Students who fasten on a form from popular fiction have a need for it; couched within the form are potential meanings they want to explore. They are like chess players, pondering infinite variables within a tight set of rules. It has been my observation that students who are encouraged to continue working within a genre as long as it engages them develop a number of narrative skills: they learn the concept of literary form and how to manipulate it; they learn cultural standards of behavior, including patterns of dialogue, and how to represent them. They learn to establish and sustain a conventional narrative stance and voice.[1]

It has also been my observation that these young writers of popular genre begin after a time to strain at the limits of the system. As their reading experience becomes wider, not to mention their personal knowledge of the world, the undeviating constructs of popular genre cease to be felt as safe and become, instead, confining. The same issues may continue to appear in their stories, but the structures gradually melt away to allow a more flexible and more personal narrative shape to evolve.

Transcending the Limits of Popular Genre: The Story of Fax

As an eighth grader, Michael, one of my "Dungeons and Dragons" enthusiasts, won admiration for a long, complex tale told from the point of view of a wizard. The story adhered closely to the genre in its quasi-medieval setting, stock characters, and the problem of overcoming a personified evil. When I picked up his newest story a year later, the first several paragraphs led me to expect more of the same. Certainly his fascination with wizards had not changed; his text picks up with the same sorts of implicit questions of meaning that last year's wizard evoked: In what lies the magic that makes a man wise? What is the nature of knowledge? What is the power of wisdom, and what are its responsibilities? True, in this story Michael has distanced himself from the wizard by employing a third-person narrator, suggesting a more objective approach to meaning, but it wasn't until I reached the end of the fifth paragraph that I realized we were dealing with a whole new concept of wizard:

> Fax stared deeply into the water filled glass. He absorbed its serenity, becoming the jewel that was floating within the holy liquid. He could feel slight tingles and mellow currents flow through him, just as the bright red crystal was affected.

---

[1] I am grateful to Anne Turvey for sharing with me her classroom research in adolescent genre writing. Her work supported and clarified these concepts drawn from my own observations.

Fax felt his physical body shift, then he realized that his spirit was leaving his body behind for the freedom of the crystal, floating in the water. Flying through the air, he passed through the wall of the glass. It was pleasant to glide through the cool water, creating ripples. Like a bird he sailed slowly, and entered the crystal's warm embrace.

The crystal brightened as it grew whole, and radiated its energy to encompass the entire glass, and illuminate the space beyond. It was comfortable and relaxing for Fax to explore the sensations within the crystal.

Suddenly Fax felt a new presence, a sharp and biting one that promised further power. This was what he was looking for, an answer to the problem he faced. It shared the space with Fax inside the crystal then imploded into a tight thing, to be held within Fax.

Fax felt a new urgency, a will to do and accomplish. Simultaneously the life force of the crystal felt a loss, as he had done before, Fax would leave it. Eager, he sailed forward, leaving the crystal and the glass behind, and piercing his vacant body. New life animated him and he turned to the silent man that sat beside him. Fax answered his question and accepted his fortune telling fee and watched the customer step out of the small, plain tent.

—*Michael, 14*

Here is a wizard who has been wrenched out of his genre and transplanted into a modern American amusement park. It is not the wizard who has changed—nor, as we shall see, the life-and-death gravity of the dilemma that he faces. What has changed is a realization on the part of the author that in twentieth-century America wizards don't have quite the status they once enjoyed. Instead of illustrating that knowledge is more powerful than evil, which is the hard-won but inevitable role of a "Dungeons and Dragons" wizard, Fax delivers the double message that knowledge is its own reward and knowledge equals responsibility equals sacrifice. Fax has special abilities that set him apart from others, but no special privileges; burdened with his knowledge, he walks unremarked about the amusement park, wishing he could enjoy its ordinary pleasures as part of the crowd:

For the first time in days he retired from his post at his tent to wander about the amusement park. It was a busy time in the day, near afternoon. Fax smelled hot dogs, fried dough, and other sweet treats. People brushed by him as they would in the city. He would have felt good to be part of the public, if it weren't that he had more pressing matters to think about.

In the modern world, as in the distant world of knights and dragons, it is the job of the wizard to use his powers for the good of others. Fax has foreseen the death of a child on a carnival ride gone out of control. No personified evil faces him, as in the genre stories; he will not have the satisfaction of defeating an enemy. Evil is entering his world, as it tends to do in this century, strictly by chance. One of those rides that's supposed to be fun suddenly turns deadly. Nor will he save a kingdom by sacrificing himself—only a child. His deed will win him no renown. Conceived and nurtured in genre, the wizard has outgrown both the safety and the restriction of its boundaries, as Michael accepts a challenge removed one giant step closer from fantasy to reality. Fax does not hesitate:

> The father motioned for his daughter to take the remaining swing. The ride began to hum, and start up. The girl moved to the seat, smoothing her dress out to keep it neat while she sat down. Fax lurched forward and past the girl. He took the swing and strapped himself in tightly.
>
> "Hey buddy, would you mind letting my daughter have that swing? You can go next time around."
>
> Fax replied painfully "I'm sorry. It–its important that I ride now. Maybe you would like to go next time with your daughter . . . On me?"
>
> Fax seemed to choke and the air got hot as he pressed some money into the man's hand and looked at the disappointed girl. Reluctantly, they agreed to Fax's terms.
>
> The girl and her father watched as the ride began its spinning. Fax relaxed, proud that he had prevented the accident and watched the scenes flying past all around him. He became entranced, mesmerized by the dizziness and spinning. The ride accelerated and lost control, all of which Fax was only partly aware of. And Fax realized that this was his noblest vision.
>
> —*Michael, 14*

Practical Matters

Short story is an excellent basic genre to encourage in student reading and writing, a stepping stone between popular genres and "serious" literature. Teenagers understand its conventions and like its length. Fine models, rich and diverse in content, are readily available, including many by female and minority writers who may not yet be accessible in the larger canon. For many of my students, short story is the first teacher-introduced genre they embrace.

Our local Vermont genre, The Hunt, first showed up in connection with Richard Connell's classic short story, "The Most Dangerous Game." As part of their response to this story, I ask students to write a page in their journal titled "The Hunt," "The Hunter," or "Hunting." Myriad versions of the same basic story result, most of them intense in tone and longer than required.

But, like all good literature, "The Most Dangerous Game" serves the cause of learning in numerous other ways. Written during the reign of Stalin, it presents in General Zaroff a perfectly evil Russian villain, who invites discussion of stereotyping. It raises ecological issues. In literary terms, this same narrative is a showcase for the three major types of conflict. It models plot development, foreshadowing, suspense, setting, and theme with a succinct clarity that adolescents are able to comprehend and incorporate into their own writing.

We read several good, provocative short stories, followed by journal writing and discussion. Some stories that have been particularly successful are London's "To Build a Fire," Wright's "Almost a Man," Olson's "Tell Me A Riddle," Bradbury's "The Screaming Woman," and Stockton's "The Lady or the Tiger?".

Next I ask students to write a short story of their own. They usually have four or five weeks to do this, with two homework nights and one computer-room session per week to work on it, plus two or three periods toward the end for conferences. There is no length requirement, though students ask for one, because

I've found by experience that the stories are freer and more various without limits. Occasionally a less confident student prefers to write two or more short scenes or anecdotes instead of a complete story.

Each story is dicussed in conference with three or four classmates. I ask conference partners to identify and discuss the effectiveness of these main story elements: plot, including rising action and climax; setting; character; and conflict. More advanced students take pride in finding other elements such as foreshadowing, symbol, and denouement.

There's no end to the range and combinations of genres my young storytellers tap for their narratives. Many of my students tell me that this is their favorite assignment of the year.

≡Seven

Cant and Canon

Reading is a creative act, whereby the individual reader uses the printed words to construct an imaginary experience. (Dixon & Stratta 1986, 397)

*I*n the high school where I teach, as in probably the majority of secondary schools in the United States, American literature is emphasized in the junior year. Our students are introduced to the fictional narratives of a familiar lineup of authors: Hawthorne, Poe, Crane, Fitzgerald, Steinbeck, Hemingway. Teachers intersperse these towering figures with works of other novelists, poets, and dramatists, as time permits, the budget stretches, and interest demands. This year I discovered to my joy that some of my students had read (and remembered with approval) several poems by Emily Dickinson. But generally we adhere pretty closely to the canon of great American literature as a framework for the course.

In an important way, the canon is a constraint: it shortchanges many splendid writers, most of them women or minority authors. In a different way, it is a blessing. Our students have the opportunity to engage with a subset of writers whose works challenge and enrich their understanding of the world. Scrambling through dusty shelves in the English department storage room, seeking to stretch the canon's boundaries with a short story by Tillie Olson or a poem by Langston Hughes, I am brought up short to find an old SRA reading program whose authors, artistic worth, and pedagogic value seem equally obscure. Such programs washed out of our school district with a fortunate ideological tide a dozen or more years ago, but they remain attractive to many public schools bound to achieve accountability. In the meantime, my students are permitted the luxury of expanding their language skills within a challenging cognitive framework: that is, they are encouraged to read and respond to great literature. And even though the choice of authors represents a cultural bias, their works possess the universality to transcend time and place, to challenge the students' assumptions about life and engage them with larger human issues.

The Canon as the Basis for Creativity and Growth

It is in their responses to canonical and "canon-worthy" literature that I find the richest evidences of creativity, linguistic development, and cognitive growth in my students. The texts are difficult, no question; adolescents without background in the conventions of an alien or centuries-old cultural tradition must delve to get inside the experiences that tradition offers. But after years of seeing it happen, I know that the best in literature has the power to call forth the best in its readers. Teenagers, even the coolest and most cynical among them, are idealists. They believe and want evidence to show that their world is worthy of their effort and respect. When the evidence is there, and they can recognize it as such, they rise eagerly to meet it.

Probably the largest single challenge facing an English teacher is to create a classroom climate in which great literature comes to life. One of the first steps is to help students realize that a revered author is really no more than somebody telling a good story. Another is to make the classroom a place where narrative abounds, a place that respects and values stories that the students themselves read and write and share. The great authors don't suffer when they are read side by side with popular books and the students' own stories; on the contrary, they're in good company. A class steeped in narrative is predisposed to accept tales from anywhere and to treat them as important windows into knowledge.

Once students have performed the creative act of reading that brings the story into their own imaginative experience, they need a wealth of possibilities for response. It is at this point—too soon in the assimilation process — that many high school teachers make the mistake of asking for cognitive closure, formal analysis, or both. A great narrative sets much more stirring in a student's head than the answers to an array of comprehension questions at the end; it evokes questions whose answers have to be reforged in every generation. One important kind of response is the critical essay, but it will be a better paper if story comes first.

For the majority of young readers, the most effective means to get a grip on a story is to relive it in some personally significant way (see chapter 5). Another important type of response, which I want to emphasize in this chapter, is to internalize the work and transform some aspects of it — themes, images, symbols — into the bedrock of a completely original narrative. When this happens, it is magic; no linguistic theory yet developed can explain the complex processes by which comprehension takes the form, not of generalization or synthesis, but of invention. It is a matter of deep calling unto deep, a reverberation below consciousness between author and reader. This communion cuts across cultural boundaries and builds webs of fundamental human understanding.

Hemingway as Inspiration

I first saw a creative response to literature on a frequent basis in American Lit classes. My rural Vermont students usually respond more positively to Hemingway than to any other canonical American author. These teenagers belong to a laconic culture: the stereotypical image of the old-time Vermonter as someone who says little except "Ay-yeh" and "Nope" is often not far from the mark. Therefore they have a hard time articulating their profound understanding of Hemingway, which is more a matter of feelings than of intellect. The imaginary experience they construct in reading him is so close to their actual experience that they have trouble distancing themselves enough to be analytical. Like Hemingway's heroes, they respect action above speech, and they value the same solitary or independent pursuits: hunting, fishing, working, fighting for a cause.

The first year I taught *In Our Time*, I was frustrated by my students' apparent inability to translate their satisfaction with the stories into conceptual statements, even after they had engaged in a number of reenactment activities. One day well along in the unit, after they had read most of the stories in the text, I greeted them with an unscheduled assignment:

> Write a story in homage to Hemingway. You may do it any way you like. You may write a story that would fit into this book, using the Nick Adams character, or write something totally different, just as long as it's done in the spirit of Hemingway. You may write a serious story or a parody. I don't want you to *think* a long time about it; just plunge in and write whatever *feels* right.

About half the students in the class produced narratives that were clearly imitations. These were what I had hoped for, and they did prove valuable in their own right as a bridge between reading and analysis of Hemingway's work. The other students went beyond mimesis to create something far richer than my expectations. Lisa, for example, wrote this little narrative, which hauled Hemingway into a new generation, not to mention a whole new cultural setting:

> Joe watched the fish weave in and out of the coral. It lived in a world of grasses and corals. There was the black coral that would be deadly if the fish ate it, and red coral that would make the fish sick and weak if it cut the fish in any way. The fish had swum into the middle of a hummock and could not figure how to get out. It was surrounded on three sides by the coral with no "safe" way out. It swam aimlessly in circles with intensifying frenzy. It was getting closer to the jagged red coral. If the fish didn't get out soon it would die of fright.
>
> As Joe watched this, he looked at his watch to find that he had five minutes to get back to the Catholic school before he would be missed. The lake was off limits to them during the week, but he just couldn't resist the temptation of going to watch the fish.

As he ran down the hill and through the meadow, he could feel his heart beating in his head. If Sister Mary Josephine discovered him missing, he would be working off the demerits she would give him for the rest of his years at the school. She always seemed to catch people right in the middle of something and punish them severely. If he was lucky, he would run into Sister Madeleine. She would give him a lecture, but that wouldn't last forever. He could live with that.

—Lisa, 16

Lisa's story adopts, internalizes, and transforms Hemingway's fatalistic attitude, his dread of constraint, and a favorite metaphor: the fish as alter ego. But it does much more. In just three paragraphs (the first time I gave this assignment, I allowed too little time to write), she establishes character, theme, conflict, and a colorful, concrete natural setting. The reader can see the red and black of the coral, the implied blue of the lake and green of the meadow. Also implied is the black-and-white austerity of the Sisters awaiting him at the school.

This contrast between the natural world and the school points up the paradoxical similarity of the fish's dilemma and Joe's. We see the fish's "intensifying frenzy" and Joe's "heart beating in his head." In this story, natural things are off-limits, and therefore, in the Catholic context, sinful: Joe "just couldn't resist the *temptation*" to visit the lake. And what bubble of experience or memory, floating to the surface of Lisa's mind as she sat at her desk in a public school, contained the image of a parochial school? We had recently seen a film of "Soldier's Home"; perhaps the repressively religious mother in this Hemingway story triggered some association. Notice that there is no redemption, either for Joe in witnessing the fish or for the fish itself; both will be lucky to come out of their respective dangers bearing a level of damage they can "live with."

Taking root in a world of Lisa's imagination, Hemingway's visions inspired hers; the resulting story, brief and unpolished though it may be, stands on its own as a piece of literature. Furthermore, when I asked Lisa and her classmates to justify the thematic and stylistic choices in the stories they had written, they were able to make the shift from narrative to the analytical language that had eluded them earlier. Lisa readily recognized the fish as a symbol once *she* had used it as such; she was able also to formulate the thematic concept, so important to Hemingway, that "nature is dangerous too, but at least it's not trying to hurt you the way people try to hurt you."

Stories Built Upon Stories: The Canon as Source

Our culture has a long and splendid tradition of art inspired by the art of others: look at *The Jew of Malta* and *The Merchant of Venice* for an obvious example. Of course *The Merchant of Venice* owes other sources as well; it is one of the glories of Shakespeare that he can weave together numerous literary threads into something transcendent and totally new. Just as the Renaissance was beginning to bring classical and European stories to England, Shakespeare was reading and absorbing as many of them as he could lay his hands on. He plumbed deep into the literature he knew, both ancient and contemporary, for ideas, characters, or whole plots. Then when he wrote his plays, he incorporated these elements into his own broad vision of the world, thus reinventing and transforming them.

Lisa, in her homage to Hemingway, was doing essentially the same thing Shakespeare did in response to Marlowe. All stories of the imagination — ALL — imitate, rewrite, or take their inspiration from stories that have gone before; each new fiction is both a creation and a re-creation. The newly invented story, whether Lisa's or Shakespeare's, is structured from its very heart on particular cultural conventions of narrative, but at the same time it reflects the unique individual consciousness of the author.[1] As Culler observes, "Literary works never lie wholly within the codes that define them," and I have found that the more a work of "literature . . . undermines, parodies, and escapes anything which threatens to become a rigid code or explicit

---

[1] Jerome Bruner's entire book, *Acts Of Meaning* (Cambridge, MA: Harvard University Press, 1990), is a superb study of the balance between cultural influences and individual meaning-making in narrative discourse.

rules for interpretation" (Culler 1976, 105), the more fertile my students are likely to find it as a ground for their own creative efforts. By and large, it is the greatest works, many of which compose the canon of a culture, that do most both to define and to "escape" the social structure; it is these works that best serve both to ground young readers in a culture and to provide them the framework for questioning its values and mores.

In America, there is really no reason anymore to see the canon as the privileged property of a cultural (or intellectual) elite. Free public education in a dynamic democratic nation can, and should, go much further than simply training children to function within their society. It should guarantee every child the opportunity to grapple with the greatest, broadest, and most enriching artistic achievements the world's cultures have to offer. These ideas are not new, of course. I was somewhat taken aback, in reading excerpts from the British Newbolt Report (published in 1921), to find impassioned pleas that I could have written myself for a literature-rich education:

> An education of this kind is the greatest benefit which could be conferred upon any citizen of a great state, and . . . the common right to it, the common discipline and enjoyment of it, the common possession of the tastes and associations connected with it, would form a new element of national unity, linking together the mental life of all classes by experiences which have hitherto been the privileges of a limited section. . . . If we use English literature as a means of contact with great minds, a channel by which to draw upon their experience with profit and delight, and a bond of sympathy between the members of a human society, we shall succeed. . . . (Mathieson 1987, 184)

Liberal and Conservative Attacks on the Canon

It seems that the Newbolt Committee and I share towards education an idealistic stance that is forever bumping into realities. On the one hand, schools are asked to provide leadership, flexibility, and the ability to guide society into the future; on the other they are expected to turn out willing workers and good citizens to uphold society's traditions. One continuing, unfortunate way schools react to these pressures is to split their students into "tracks" in which only the academically gifted encounter fine literature. Even for those lucky few, access to the canon is in ideological danger. Another is to pursue some academic fast-food philosophy that levels all students in a wasteland of intellectual burgers and fries. There are currently two strands of thought in education, one postmodern and one reactionary, that reflect these conflicting ideologies, and both of which militate against teaching the canon. Both, to some degree, are dangerous to our children.

The classics of English-American literature have fallen into serious disrepute in the last couple of decades among learning theorists, literary critics, and social scientists. Illogically, scholars protest on the one hand against the impossibility of defining the canon as a specific body of works, and on the other against its particular characteristics as the purveyor of a dominant white Anglo-American male power structure. Numerous studies (Wald 1989, Pace 1992, for example) show an overwhelming percentage of white male authors represented in current American literature anthologies, although as Wald notes, "Merely to talk as if there exists in the United States a single, only moderately differentiated, clearly identifiable literature or culture is a dangerously misleading simplification . . . " (1989, 5).

In the face of rising feminism and multicultural awareness, the canon appears to be at best outdated, at worst oppressive. And yet it is my "politically incorrect" opinion that these scholars who would do away with the canon in the schools are throwing out the baby with the bath water. In attempting to right historic wrongs, they are willing to deny the best narrative and poetry that their culture has produced. After all, it is the richness, diversity, beauty, and challenge of individual works in the canon that beguiled most of us into teaching English in the first place. One of the goals of English teachers has historically been to share some of that literary glory for students of the next generation. I believe that this remains a worthy goal.

On the other end of the scale, educators who reject great literature to embrace "teacher-proof," outcome-oriented, prepackaged reading programs are guiltier than those who teach the canon of perpetuating an outdated elitist image of their culture (de Castell and Luke 1989, 78). In the eyes of overly conservative educators, literature geared to a bygone century or a lofty intellectual level is irrelevant to their pedagogic mission. These teachers are so intent on defining and "going back to" basics that they lose sight of the educational riches beyond the basics. They are preparing children to possess life skills and hold jobs, to maintain the status quo and be evaluated for how well they adhere to its structure. They are not preparing children to grow; to expand their horizons; to question, participate in, lead, and change their society to meet the future.

Canon vs. Genre

Theme vs. Formula So how are we to view the canon? Is it representative of the finest, most transcendent literary works of a culture, or is it conservator of the values and especially the power of a social elite? Of course it is both, and therefore worthy of both praise and censure; most of all, it is worthy of emendation and expansion as our understandings of literary achievement grow with our acceptance of social complexity. Another of our goals as English teachers should be to maintain a critically receptive stance toward a wide range of literature, to know and love and offer to students the finest books written by women, Native Americans, African Americans, writers in other languages, and minority authors as well as the familiar Anglo-American white male authors. If "the canon" is going to continue to be synonymous with "the best," then it can't remain static; it will have to embrace a broader cultural base.

It's tricky, of course, to determine "best" outside the old parameters. Many schools don't make much effort: they may opt for the safety of traditional anthologies, or worse, for the sterile lessons of a basal reading series, such as the program that gave me pause in my explorations of the department archives. These carefully structured texts emphasize the acquisition of discrete skills rather than personal interaction with literary content, which, as de Castell and Luke warn, leads to "the development in both teacher and student of an uncritical and mechanical relation to the reading of text, the writing of text and the acquisition of knowledge from text" (1989, 84).

Although teachers in general are uncomfortable with genre novels, many schools—acknowledging, at least, the need to diversify their reading curriculum—have adopted them for classroom use because they appeal to reluctant readers and contribute to discipline. In a television culture, popular literature seems more relevant to students' lives than does the traditional literary text. It is true, as I have argued already, that genre novels are a valid stepping-off point for student narrative writers, but as subjects of study they do not replace the great works of literature, from which they differ intrinsically.

Although the lines are blurred, one helpful way to distinguish "genre" from "canon" (or, more accurately, "canon-worthy" literature) is to examine the themes of the work. There are great works of literature that survive from century to century and from culture to culture because their themes are universal, common to all human beings. Christopher Clausen calls these themes "timeless," and he goes on to define a timeless theme as

a permanently plausible interpretation of mortal questions . . . one that reminds us forcefully of the basic conditions of human life—its aspirations and limits. Those conditions are larger and deeper than any culture or historical period. The broadest context that all men and women share is an ambiguous world into which we are born helpless; in which we love, hate, struggle, and suffer; in which we grow older and die. All cultures interpret these irreducible facts, often in strikingly different ways, but no culture can change them. For human beings, they are universal in the strictest sense. (1991, 208-9, emphasis in original)

It may be said that all works of literature, not just the greatest ones, deal with universal "irreducible facts" because they all deal with human beings. A teen romance and *Romeo and Juliet* are both about forbidden young love, for example. But this is the subject, not the theme. In the teen romance, boy and girl meet in a strictly limited twentieth-century context, face the prohibitions that American high school culture dictates, and overcome them in ways that satisfy not only their own desires but those of traditional teachers, parents, and peers. No important questions remain at the end of the book. A statement of the theme of such a romance would have to include the cultural context in which it was produced. What makes *Romeo and Juliet* endure to fascinate each new batch of freshmen, six thousand miles and four centuries removed from its creation, is the way Shakespeare opens up a world of speculation about burningly important "mortal questions" that attach to forbidden young love: issues such as family and peer loyalty, authority, prejudice, and the nature of love itself. Different societies and historical periods might state the theme of *Romeo and Juliet* differently according to their own perspectives, but its universal quality lies in the questions it raises, asking each culture and each reader to wrestle with their own answers.

Open vs. Closed   The concept that Shakespeare opens up questions is an important one. Another way to look at works of "genre" versus "canon" is to consider the former "closed" and the latter "open" texts (Eco 1979 as cited by de Castell and Luke 1989). Closed texts such as romances, mysteries, and "Dungeons and Dragons" "require minimal participation from the reader.... They represent limited 'causal chains' operating, like TV narratives, on the basis of wholly predictable narrative structures... " whereas the open text "challenges and expands known schematic structures and thereby requires... 'higher order' abilities of comprehension and interpretation. *Such texts require a systematic rewriting on the part of the reader...* " (de Castell and Luke 1989, 90, emphasis mine).

There are many ways to "rewrite a text" effectively; creating an original narrative inspired by the text is only one of them, and a fairly specialized one at that. In the years since Lisa wrote her Hemingway story, I have continued to encourage students to write their own narratives in response to works of the canon, the greatest and often the most difficult works of literature English teachers offer their classes. These works are difficult because by definition they are open, multidimensional; no one reading of them is "right," just as no one classroom approach is sure to make them accessible. Conversation, journal writing, film, dramatization and improvisation, paraphrasing, textual analysis, and artistic interpretation are all useful forms of "rewriting" a complex narrative text. Even when the teacher is an expert, no class can successfully rely on a single approach to literature that invites multiple readings.

Creativity in Reading and Responding to Great Literature

Many teachers, educated in a different era, caught between a deep love of language and a practical need for student assessment, send their classes mixed messages about the canon. Consider, for example, Shakespeare, the ultimate canonic author. How many English teachers present him to their students as some kind of golden icon, a being to be held in awe, whose genius is so far above their little lives that they have no hope of bringing him to life? I was guilty in this way of ruining Shakespeare for twenty-two unhappy sophomores the first time I tried to teach *A Midsummer Night's Dream*; their disenchantment caused sleepless nights and sent me on a quest to learn how to do better. On the other hand, how many English teachers offer Shakespeare as just another (admittedly tough) text to be decoded, carved up into vocabulary lists and comprehension questions, and tested, thus guaranteeing that a few kids will get A's and the rest will hate Shakespeare? Worst of all, how many English teachers, when the crunch comes, find Shakespeare too outdated and too difficult for *their* kids, and leave him on the shelf? Teachers who have the privilege of teaching great works have also the responsibility first to facilitate a meeting between those works and students, then to *get out of the way* while students and author together "create an imaginative experience."

If to read a story is to create and imagine, might not one valid response to reading be creative and imaginative as well? I find it hard to understand why American high schools work so diligently to cut students off from their own creative impulses. It's almost a holy mission, a conscious, systematic putting away of childish things. For American adolescents, creativity suddenly becomes the province of young children and geniuses, with no bridge across the gap. Somewhere off in a far wing of the building, they can take an art course, sing or play an instrument; maybe they can choose a semester of "creative writing," even some drama if they're lucky and the school is well endowed. But this is merely constructive play, not the serious business of schooling.

The core classes, the ones that Get You Into College or Prepare You For Life, insist that someone else was the only worthwhile creator. They send the message that students who are at last mature enough to engage the truly great artistic (or scientific, or social) minds of their culture are best occupied in absorbing their wisdom. It is the student's job to accept and echo, not evaluate and create. Also, it is too often true in our schools that great minds are replaced by not-always-wise "adult experts" who produce textbooks or reading programs, but the requirements for the student do not change. In the latter case, the student, twice removed from any wellspring of creativity—her own or the author's—finds school an irrelevant bore.

Of course it's important for students to learn how to analyze a piece of literature. They should certainly be able to recognize and describe structural elements, to develop and support arguments about the meaning of a work, and to generalize from the author's ideas. These are valid goals of a high school education — but to a ninth grader who, with considerable effort, has just succeeded in reading (imaginatively creating) Odysseus's encounter with the Cyclops, they are pretty dry. The *Odyssey*, like most canonical works, touches off fundamental resonances in the reader. It makes a lot of sense to let the student first respond to Homer story for story.

Reading and Responding to Homer: Student Odysseys   One of my favorite assignments for ninth graders follows their reading of extensive excerpts from the *Odyssey*. The prompt is very simple: "You are to write a personal odyssey. It may be factual or fictional. It must include a main character who makes some sort of journey, either actual or metaphoric, during which he or she has adventures and learns something. Over the next several weeks you will be given homework time and computer lab time in which to write your odyssey and class time in which to discuss it in conference."

The range of responses to this assignment has been amazing. Students of all ability levels embrace Homer—the magic, the heroism, the human extravagance of his work shows up by a linguistic alchemy in theirs. Most of my freshman students have never before read a work as spiritually and physically large as the *Odyssey*, and most have never before been asked to complete such an open-ended and long-range writing assignment. During the final day in the computer lab, I am filled with anticipation as the stack of finished odysseys grows in my hands. I have watched them take shape as the weeks have gone by, read bits on the computer screens over my students' shoulders, offered advice to one who gets stuck and a sympathetic ear to another who needs to talk through ideas, eavesdropped here and there on conferences; but even after all my participation in the process, I find few moments in teaching to match the surprise and delight of that first night's pre-evaluative reading.

I can never predict which student is going to reflect back which aspects of Homer's genius. There is an intense sort of communication that occurs between bard and student. Bakhtin writes, "The unique speech experience of each individual is shaped and developed in continuous and constant interaction with others' individual utterances. This experience can be characterized to some degree as the process of *assimilation*—more or less creative—of others' words . . . " (1986, 89, emphasis in original). The desire to respond to Homer, to carry on a dialogue three thousand years old about how to get where you're going, is compelling for many students, who become caught up in a powerful narrative drive. Stacey, who wrote a longer and more complex story than anything she had ever attempted before, gave a fine subjective description of the narrative process in her evaluation: "I'm not sure how it [my story] developed, I just kept up my head and kept pumping ideas to my fingers and they appeared on the screen."

I want to close this chapter with the introductory sections of two student odysseys, including Stacey's. I chose these two because they give a good sense of how communion with a great author results in bursts of comprehension and creativity unique to each individual. Both young authors homed in on several of the same themes and images from the *Odyssey*, but each developed and maintained through several thousand words a personal voice completely different from the other.

"Last Odyssey"

Everyone boarded the old rickety ship and dallied along to their quarters (boards squeaking) knowing what a long trip this was going to be.

"All Aboard! First stop Cactus Island!"

Everyone knew that when the Captain said, "Cactus Island," that peace talks were the furthest thing from his mind. The Captain was known as a cold hearted man with a passion for a bloody battle.

I was nervous, this was the second "ship adventure," as the captain liked to call it, and I knew what to expect. I remembered my first adventure last year. When I watched all the people I had become friends with get killed, I swore that I would never let my father sign me up again. My father was a marine until he was injured in the Vietnam War. When I was a boy, he would sit me down after dinner and tell me one of his many stories about how he helped save our country. His stories fascinated me and because of them I was determined to be just like my dad.

I felt the tug as the ship pulled away from the docks. Everyone was waving goodbye to their families, everyone except me. My family wasn't there to say goodbye because they didn't believe in goodbyes. My mom always said that goodbyes were for the people who had no respect for God, because any person who believed in the Lord had to believe that they would see the ones they lost, when they reached heaven.

— Stacey, 14

In this somber opening scene of Stacey's adventure tale, it is clear how deeply the mythical messages of the *Odyssey* have permeated her consciousness. She begins by showing her narrator embarking on an ocean voyage that ruptures him from his family.

There is deliberate ambiguity in the line, "I felt the tug as the ship pulled away from the docks," as the narrator breaks away to begin a journey both spiritual and physical. Like Odysseus's trip, its background is the memory of a war that was fought heroically and patriotically, but that created an uneasy situation at home. The narrator is caught between loyalty to his father and loathing for his bloodthirsty captain (which is surely how Odysseus must have appeared, at least sometimes, to the doomed men of his crew). The voyage will be filled with unnamed dangers. Above it lurks a problematic God who guarantees no earthly salvation.

Stacey sees the *Odyssey* in terms of adventure, mortal danger, and human frailty in the face of circumstance. Jonathan sees it as a romp. His main character also takes off over the sea into a world of fabulous dangers, but the third-person narrator's attitude recalls the cockiness of Odysseus and the humor that is characteristic of his response to peril. Like Stacey, Jonathan invokes god(dess) and family and the overt threat of death, but it is done with a joyous exuberance of language that Homer himself might enjoy:

Tuna Fish and All
Prologue
As the magic carpet sped over the choppy water towards land, the figure, perched on the center of the carpet, hanging on for dear life, was alternately screaming prayers and curses, "Oh great merciful mother don't let me fall," then he would shout, "Dam it all, if mother finds out That I was flying over the ocean again she'll tan my hide!" He continued to shout prayers and curses out loud as he raced the storm, like a huge grey steed, across the sky, the sea beneath him getting steadily wilder and wilder, at one point a high swell touched the bottom of the torn, threadbare carpet with it's white salty spume.

Suddenly a strong gust of wind, combined with a now average swell of forty feet tossed the old bedraggled carpet tassle over tassle into the churning water among the jagged off shore rocks which thrust upwards like a perverse statuary of the dead. He sank under the white foamy surface not knowing he was about to be thrown, willing or not into the strangest adventure of his young life.

—Jonathan, 14

Stacey and Jonathan took a risk in writing their odysseys, launching their own innovative narrative responses to a wonderfully bold ancient storyteller. This open writing assignment following a challenging reading assignment is not successful with all students, although I am always pleased by how many come through. Some need more structure; some need to nibble away at new ideas in smaller bites. With these students I negotiate individually until we agree on a structure with which we are both comfortable.

Teenagers trying out their own ideas like the security of a predictable narrative form. Even after being introduced to a piece of literature that challenges and excites them, and even when their concerns push against closed conventions, they often choose to write their own stories within the structural framework of a current popular genre. This is a natural, acceptable stage of growth, but student writing, like student reading, should keep pushing towards more complex and challenging levels. English teachers do their students the greatest service by opening up to them the world of moral, social, and artistic conjecture. Their primary task is to make the richest, most complex works of literature accessible and vital to adolescents who are more comfortable snuggled up to TV sitcoms or Stephen King. Most English teachers therefore should and do embrace "the canon" with all its flaws, at the same time constantly seeking to expand its cultural boundaries.

Practical Matters

It's an interesting challenge to read some of the more difficult works of the canon with a heterogeneously grouped class. The academically advanced students tend to gobble them up, often to react superficially and then grow bored as those with less developed skills struggle through. One simple technique I've found helpful is to "Divide and Conquer".

Instead of assigning the same set number of pages to be read by all students at the same time, I divide the passage into short sections and assign each student a section to rehearse and read aloud. Sometimes the rehearsal is done for homework; more

often I give it ten minutes or so at the beginning of class. Sometimes I ask my students to prepare individually by subvocalizing—that is, by shaping the words silently with their mouths while hearing them in their minds. This is an excellent technique to promote awareness and appreciation of the sounds of words. More often, though, I pair a weaker with a stronger student to practice aloud together. The academically gifted (who will have read the passage already) and the very restless students may be sent off to prepare an improvisation of the most dramatic section of the passage. When the class reassembles, the students read their passages aloud by turn, and then they witness or participate in a reenactment of the scene.

I save the "Divide and Conquer" technique for passages that are particularly difficult, dramatic, or crucial to the narrative. There are at least three good outcomes: virtually all students have the experience of reading aloud successfully; most pay careful attention to the reading of their classmates because, having read only a small section of the scene, they want to find out what happens; and the class as a whole experiences an important part of the story.

≡*Eight*

Autobiographical Writing: "Inventing the Truth"

... one of my favorite things is to hear other people's works. Stories are one of those things I can never get enough of.

— *Kathy, 17*

It was dark outside, and very humid. I could feel a thick mist around me. It hugged me tighter than the darkness yet still a cold grip. I wanted to put my hands inside my pockets, where I knew they would be warm. Instead I continued to feel my way across the aluminum roof outside my window. The roof creaked and popped under me, despite the way I had spread my weight across all fours. Too much noise. The aluminum was wet and I was afraid my boots would slip, but I did not want to set my knees down and dampen them. Finally I reached the corner of the flat roof, where it met the shorter roof of what had been an outhouse sometime long ago. The crickets chirped and paused, as if they heard me when I made a sound. I was afraid someone had heard me leaving, but even if they did hear me it would no longer matter. I remained perched there for a while, staring into the black clouds around me. I heard the dog shift at the end of the chain. I hoped that my cat Lily was not around. I would miss her and to hear her call would break me. Imagining it was bad enough.

I looked down to where I thought the ground was and went through the jump/landing/roll in my mind. If only the moon was out, or a breeze blowing, or something else natural to tell me that I myself was acting within nature. I would miss this old house. I began to weep. I would miss all of it. I tried to stop crying with thoughts of things I didn't like here, but found that I would miss them too. I jumped, purposely not paying attention and landing sloppily. The soft pain in my shoulder helped the tears go away.

For an instant I hated what I was doing. But I had to move on, and I wanted to leave hate behind me.

—*Michael, 16*

I was sitting by the fire hydrant on the corner of Smith and Hamilton Street. It was damp outside, and the pavement was wet. Water had soaked through my clothes, cooling my skin.

I felt a hand touch my shoulder, and I was afraid to turn around. I was afraid to move. Whose ever hand it was had chapped skin, but was very gentle. I slowly picked my head up and stared into the man's eyes.

He was dressed in blue, and his badge created a reflection that made me blink and turn away. His eyes were like mirrors. He looked very annoyed. His skin and his hair were very white, and he almost glowed in the dark.

He instructed me to get into his car. It smelled like coffee; cups were rattling around. The leather on the back seat was cold, and I could hardly see anything through the wire cage. There were very few people in sight. The ones I did see were dressed warmly and were singing around garbage cans with continuous flames coming out of them. Someone made a remark to the officer that I didn't understand. I remember frowning, and the officer peered at me through his mirror.

I wasn't crying, and I hardly felt anything. The officer spoke to me in a very deep voice. I answered the questions without hesitating. I told him I hadn't eaten in two days. The hunger pains had drifted away after a while. The only light came from the dash board and the street lights.

This section of town had very terrible houses, but I didn't notice. I was starting to think about my father, and what he was going to say. I was afraid he would hurt me and never forgive me for leaving. The officer seemed to know where he was going, he hadn't asked me my name or where I lived. He turned into my street, and I could see a shadowy figure sitting on the concrete steps to my house. Were they waiting for me? Did they miss me? Questions raced through the gears in my head. I only missed some parts about my parents. I didn't miss my sister at all.

The officer took a left hand turn into my driveway, and the oil spots glowed in the headlights. My father stood up as the cruiser pulled in. The officer parked slightly crooked. I was slouching in the back seat. I'm not sure if my father could see me. I could see him in his jeans and undershirt. His undershirts were always stained with funny colors. The officer stepped out of the car and one foot slipped on the black top. He opened the door, and held out his hand. I climbed out of the car and all I could do was stand there.

My father started to cry at the sight of me. I let one tear go and fought with myself. I keep telling myself to stay strong. My father had been sweating. I could tell because his hair was drenched.

The officer drove away and neither of us noticed him. Our eyes met and I could see the pain I had caused. I saw steam rising slowly behind him from the man hole. His arms were limp, and his knees looked as if they were locked, like a statue. I thought by running away it would be better for everybody. We were always fighting, so maybe some time alone would help. I was thankful to be home, but at the same time I was angry and hurt that they looked for me. We stood there for about ten minutes, although it felt an eternity. He started to move towards me. I think I backed away, but he hugged me with all of his might. I could feel his arms tighten and I could hear his heart beat. It started out fast, and then slowed down.

— Cathy, 16

Core Stories

Teacher-author Barry Lane says, "Everyone has 'core stories' — stories about that which has shaped your life in such a profound way that you'll tell it all your life, and maybe once you'll tell it well" (1992).

Barry, author of *Writing as a Road to Self-Discovery* (1993), has worked not only with schoolchildren but with Holocaust survivors, prisoners, and Cambodian refugees. He has helped them to "look inward, remember, reflect," and to tell their stories in order to learn the truth about who they are within the framework of what has happened to them. "Writing is a second chance. You go back to what you didn't know you knew. It doesn't really matter, the facts of the story — it's like what Joan Didion said, 'What happened is how I remember it.' Writing is Re-Vision with a capital 'R' — revision is not a *stage* of writing, it *is* writing!" (1992).

Two of the most common core stories, mythic in their universality, have to do with running away and with coming home. Many of my students, including Michael and Cathy, have chosen to deal with one or the other or both in their writing. Running away, says Barry with a laugh, "is a metaphor for where teenagers are!" Certainly it is a metaphor to Michael, who had never actually done it *except* in his stories, over and over again, through heroic flight (as in his ninth-grade story of Fax [see chapter 6]), escape to the past or the future, or death. How important to experience are facts? How often had Michael actually ventured out into the night, only to turn back? "If our dreams weren't already real within us, we couldn't even dream them" (Steinem 1992, 322). Michael's journey across the roof, realized down to the smallest detail, treads that fine line between fact and fiction where truth resides.

Homecomings, like departures, may be either poignant or bitter. Barry recalls a Holocaust survivor who lovingly told and retold stories of the house in which she had lived as a child: "This cherished memory, this place inside her that's still there—it's home. She can return there." My adolescent students like to write about a place (often the home of a grandparent, often a summer "camp" in the New England sense, a rural family retreat) where they felt safe or cared for as children. Some, the offspring of split families, write about returning to a parent they thought they'd lost.

Cathy's homecoming, in sharp contrast, is a descent into the inferno. She has no control, not even comprehension, of the messages and movements of those who govern her destiny. "Someone made a remark to the officer that I didn't understand. I remember frowning, and the officer peered at me through his mirror." This officer, the policeman who finds her, lacks human substance. He is made up of reflective surfaces (his badge, his eyes, the mirror) in which she finds herself wanting; ghostlike, he almost glows in the dark. Continuous flames rise from garbage cans about which the damned souls sing, and steam rises from a manhole, straight from hell, framing her father's "shadowy" figure. The driveway and her father's shirt are smirched with false colors and slippery with oil and sweat, foul and treacherous.

As an eight-year-old living in New York City, Cathy actually did run away. Her narrative, like Michael's, is both precise in sensory detail and carefully flat and controlled in style; but where his story drowns in regret, hers thrusts out a stiff straight arm against despair. Michael dreads hearing his cat because her love will break him; Cathy dreads seeing her father because his anger will hurt her. Both of them begin in limbo, cold, wet, smothered in darkness. Michael, leaving of his own volition, weeps; Cathy, returning without her own consent, cannot permit herself to shed a second tear. "I keep telling myself to stay strong," she says, the present verb tense a suggestive error in a careful, accurate paper. Both young authors bravely choose to confront the dark, dangerous, and lonely hollows of their lives with an unflinching clarity of vision. They (and their readers) understand both their vulnerability and their strength in doing so.

Autobiographical Narrative as Self-Discovery

"The problem of what to tell, how to understand it to tell it, and the courage required to be honest enough to tell it," says Robert Brooke, "all come together as central ingredients in the process of writing" (1991, 71).

"Self-discovery," says Barry Lane, "is self-healing" (1992).

The idea that telling one's story is a healthy, integrative act echoes again and again through the words of teachers, counselors, and psychiatrists. Psychotherapist Erving Polster even titles his book *Every Person's Life Is Worth a Novel* (1987). In the introduction he invites his readers with him "to open the covers of our own lives in order to find the marvels inside, painful or pleasurable. When we do, we move toward the *satisfactions of a confirmed existence*" (x, emphasis in original). In our cultural polyglot of a society, too often racist, too often sexist, too often competitive, how important it is to confirm the existence of *all* our children! Telling one's story heals because it makes real the experience, the voice, and the very being of the teller.

The Authority of the Autobiographical Narrator

Telling one's story does more than heal: it confers authority upon the narrator. Even in a literate society, even when the story is read instead of spoken, the narrator assumes some tattered but real remnant of the storyteller's ancient power. And because it is his own story, he assumes the status of expert, the possessor of knowledge that is his alone to share. This characteristic of endowing the individual with strength explains why narrative has come to be called—proudly by feminists, condescendingly by male scholars, erroneously in the final analysis— "women's way of knowing." Gloria Steinem points out succinctly that college women (and, I would add, adolescent girls) are disempowered by "being told we are 'subjective' if we cite our own experience; that the 'objective' truth always lies within the group—and the group is never us" (1992, 116).

But why limit the excluded "us" to women only? Why not welcome into the category of "us" blacks, Hispanics, Asians, American Indians, poor people, fat people, gays, weirdos, remedial kids, nerds, long-distance runners, teachers who get stuck with lunch duty—anyone who ever feels excluded from "the group"? Show me the teenager—*any* teenager—who isn't at least sometimes sure that "the group is never me." In the teeth of adult authority, peer pressure, academic competition, and an uncertain future looming ever closer, the adolescent is struggling at every level to negotiate both a personal and a group identity. Anything a teacher can do to help adolescent students develop self-esteem is all to the good. I don't mean the swagger and prejudice that so many adolescents adopt as a cover for insecurity, but real self-esteem, which can afford to be generous to others. And English teachers have a strong ally in autobiographical writing, because virtually all adolescents find themselves empowered by mining their own lives to find a self and a voice.

Autobiographical Writing and Community

Nor is it just the storyteller who is validated by her own narrative. A teller implies a listener, or better still, a community of listeners, drawn together into a group by the common experience of her vision. Discussing in conference and sharing are important for any writing, but they are imperative for personal narrative. Each writer in turn has the opportunity to invite peers into her life and enter into the lives of others. Positive sharing of personal narratives is the quickest way I know to develop a classroom community in which everyone (including the teacher) holds stature and respect. It is also the quickest way I know to elicit quality work, because good writing is the ticket into the group. In one way or another, I make sure that autobiographical writing is a part of every class I teach.

When I ask for student evaluations, nearly all stress the importance of the conference, and many express surprise either at the quality of the papers in general or at the respect with which their own work was received. Most feel affirmed as writers, and most observe that they have learned something about themselves. David, a senior struggling to decide whether or not to go into the risky business of dairy farming, chose for his personal writing project to tell the story of his early childhood on a dairy farm. He called up his past to inform his future. The result was a detailed, loving picture of a childhood made happy by its setting. His evaluation reflects satisfaction with both this piece of writing and the response of his classmates:

> In September, I started out writing slow and cautious. I was unsure of my writing ability. After conferencing once though, I became more confident. The students liked my writing. As a writer, I guess I have just been slowly improving.
>
> The changes occurred as I grew more confident. When my "Fire" paper [an autobiographical narrative] came back, I was pumped. It was the first good paper I had ever written.
>
> I enjoy conferencing. It is very helpful, and I like to hear other papers. Editing is a must. Most of my mistakes are grammatical errors.
>
> The best thing that I have done in the class is my personal writing. To be honest, I love that paper. Each time I read it, I relive those moments. I guess I am proud of the way I grew up.
>
> —*David, 16*

The Author's Stance in Autobiographical Writing

Autobiographical writing sounds deceptively easy—just tell what "really happened." In fact autobiography is the most complex of all narrative disciplines (except history, of which it is a branch), because neither the author nor the reader can know where fact ends and fiction begins. As the event influenced the narrator, so in retrospect does the narrator, re-viewing it through a filter made up of his unique memory and sensibility, influence the event. An important part of any story is the stance of the teller. As William Zinsser says in the provocatively titled book *Inventing the Truth*, a "searcher for truth in the buried past . . . knows that it can only be quarried by an act of imagination" (25). By choosing where to begin and end, which sensory detail to highlight here, which echo of dialogue to include there, the present self both reports and creates an experience in which the past self participated.

It has been my impression that older adolescents derive more value from writing autobiography than do younger ones. Children would generally rather write fiction. Their sense of reality is still shot through with magic and mediated with play; thus they are more comfortable adopting familiar forms of fantasy and traditional story than trying to forge some structure out of the chaos of daily living. Children are also still working on the peculiarly modern discipline of separating self from other. Often in their fictional stories, identifying with their main character, they will shift the narrator's voice from third to first person. The stories they do tell of their lives tend to be anecdotal, either events strung together without a guiding viewpoint or little snippets of experience against which to test some new idea. Children younger than about fourteen simply haven't lived long enough to distinguish who they are from who they were. Since it is only by distancing themselves from an experience that writers are able to objectify and shape it, they need to have lived long enough to establish that distance.

Older adolescents are fascinated by this new ability to stand outside themselves. It opens up all kinds of possibilities for analyzing and judging the context of their lives and their own behavior within it. As my students are just coming to understand the importance and variety of narrative viewpoint, I may ask them as an exercise to write an autobiographical story in the third person.[1] This assignment forces writers to see themselves as a character in the story of their own lives. Most students take the task very seriously, finding it both challenging and intriguing to draw themselves from the outside. Certainly there is no trouble getting involved with the subject. It always surprises me how severe adolescents are with themselves, how moral and idealistic. Some produce stories they would never have dreamed of writing in the first person; "I couldn't have," said Tracy about her narrative, which interestingly she had labelled "True Story" in the heading. This paper shocked her classmates, who saw in her, as I did, a cheerful, self-assured girl. But there is no questioning the truth of its vision.

She Hides It Well

In the corner, there was she. Her mind was an endless game full of tricks that played on her.

Her thoughts and feelings were like hundreds of conversations going on, all at once.

Her knees pressed up against her chest and her arms wrapped around them. She felt secure by giving herself a barrier that protected herself from the world that rejected her.

Solitary is what she wanted to feel, all alone within the deep thoughts that haunted her. These tricks that she played made people think that they knew her.

There was she, walking down the hallways of her school, with a smile on her face. Laughing and giggling like nothing was wrong. She shared nothing to her friends about her sadness.

People walked up to her for advice. She did the best she could. She was the healer for her friends.

She was disgusted with herself.

She had only the image that kept her happy. Her dream (that she was living) was her only survival. Her dream was her life, not her reality. . . .

---

[1] I adopted this assignment whole from David Huddle's class in fiction writing at Bread Loaf.

Figuring out what her mind was telling her was most difficult for her. Her accomplishment was to start to understand what it was really saying to her. Days on to days she attempted to understand and now she is there. No one really notices and no one really sees, because she hides it well.

— Tracy, 17

Autobiographical Writing in a Classroom Workshop

Writers in a workshop setting expand their world view and examine their own lives in light of what they learn from each other's narratives. To share a piece of writing like Tracy's opens up whole vistas of half-remembered, half-repressed experience in the minds of her listeners; stories upon stories tumble out in response. The girl who writes that she is rejected by the world suddenly finds herself accepted by — and spokesperson for — a whole group of people, each of whom has at some point felt rejected by the world. Tracy and her classmates learn something about the nature of outcasts; they may even learn to be a little more tolerant of rejects, themselves included. This is not assessable learning, to be sure. The teacher gains anyway, because day by day and story by story the class becomes more cohesive, cooperative, and engaged.

The development of a classroom community allows adolescents to take some personal risks in their writing. It is easier for a teenager who feels secure in a group to launch out and try to define himself as an individual. As he incorporates experiences from lives of others into his own world picture, the adolescent writer continues to try to locate himself in the landscape, to identify what it is that sets him apart and makes him unique. In the process, he establishes not only a point of view, which may change from story to story, but the beginnings of a voice, which is as constant and characteristic of the writer as a fingerprint.

The Development of Voice in Autobiographical Writing

The concept of voice is very complicated. It is the discourse of one person functioning within a socially defined genre; thus it is representative of both the individual and of his culture. It is not the same as style, which may change, like point of view, to meet the needs of the story or the audience. Voice, in a writer, is more synonymous with *who I am*. It incorporates background, culture, experience, and moral stance. It is appropriate for adolescents trying to discover who they are to try on different voices, and for the teacher to encourage them. But sometimes, when a student gets a piece of autobiographical writing just right, it is so transparent that *who I am* shines through the story, and the author's voice rings out. This paragraph, part of a long autobiographical narrative in the third person, was written by a senior girl, Alex (not her real name). Her childhood had been troubled; in junior high she had been, in her own words, "pretty wild." Then in freshman year came an event that changed her life — her "core story." I'm not sure whether to call it a running away or a coming home story — *finding* home, perhaps.

Excerpt from "Alex"

In the ninth grade there was a class trip to Maine. Alex fell in love with the ocean and would have stayed there if she could. She even tried, but she was discovered both times she attempted to get away. She couldn't figure out why they were keeping her trapped. She fell in love with the animals of the woods and longed to be where she was forever. She loved the ocean and loved the fact that she now knew of something that she could use to best represent her torn heart, the tides. The way they pulled in and out of the shore. Always on the go or coming in, but never the same. On the last day Alex woke up early, she was so afraid. The rain was a great disguise for her tears. She tore bare footed through the wilderness to a place she had adopted as her "own" in the short week they had been there. She had learned quickly and knew where the footing was best. When she could run no longer, she sat in the soaking ferns and let her heart break. Even with all the pain this week had brought, Alex couldn't tear herself away from it. But she had to. She hated to leave everything. It was a long bus ride back.

— Alex, 17

There is a good deal of artistry, conscious or unconscious, in Alex's narrative. An academically acculturated reader is pleased by rhythm and metaphor, and by repetitions of sound like the ones in this sentence: "When she could run no longer, she sat in the soaking ferns and let her heart break." Alex's voice is structured by American literary conventions. Her sentences echo the going out and coming in of the tides, until the last three brief, flat sentences take her away. So powerfully does she identify with the coastal wilderness that she becomes a part of it, a little barefoot animal crying rain. Even though the language may be mechanically shaky, Alex, certain of the self she discovered three years earlier in Maine, is at one with her words.

Voice is not synonymous with art, but an authentic voice possesses integrity and definition. Some writers have a voice shaped by forces markedly different from the cultural norm. Writers who spent their childhood in nonliterate cultures, for example, bring to written language a voice molded by conventions unlike those that came naturally to Alex. And a true voice reflects both the culture that shaped it and the particular qualities of an individual within that culture. It takes considerable courage and honesty, especially for an adolescent writer, to expose to the group a self that is not only unique, but also in some way at odds with the group identity.

Brandon, born and raised for his first nine years in rural Kentucky, wrote several autobiographical pieces in which he returned to his roots. Past teachers had discouraged him from exploring this funny, rustic voice, which rasps against the granite sensibilities of Vermont. An intelligent student, he had developed a properly subdued linguistic style. But a trip home to visit his grandfather loosed his tongue, to the delight of his classmates, who found Brandon's authentic voice more appealing and more acceptable than his earlier efforts to sound like the rest of them. In his evaluation he offered thanks for being allowed to write the way he wanted to. This passage from the story of his trip is typical. It picks up in a men's clothing store, where he and his Daddy while away some time until his Granddaddy arrives to take them home.

Excerpt from "Capitalist Pleasures"

The female assistant was really sweet to me and was very attractive. My Daddy told her I needed some shorts that would turn heads. She came up with some rad shorts, one fluorescent pink, the other fluorescent green. I walked into the dressing room and put them on. When I walked out I asked her, "How do they look?" She said, "Very tight and very tasteful." Daddy even said they looked good. . . .

When we got home we had a massive cookout of grits and grilled possum over a hickory chip fire. We went out back and looked over granddaddy's still. "Looks like you got it in tip top shape, Granddaddy". I said.

"A man's still is his pride and joy, sonny," he said, flashing a yellow smile. Then it was time for the camp fire.

I went over to see my neighbor across the street. "Yo, Jethro, what say you come join us for the tire fire?"

"Hey man, I ain't seen you since you was hanging with Shawn last year at Winn Dixie, what's up, Yankee?"

"We gonna have foam insulation, old tires, curtains, old gasoline, chemicals, and ddt."

"Sounds like a nice little buzz to me," Jethro said. The fire was a huge success and altogether there were five chemical explosions. It always gives me a major rush when we have flames shooting up to twenty five feet in the air.

— Brandon, 17

Practical Matters

Autobiographical writing is easily assigned in composition or creative writing classes, but what about a course in which the primary emphasis is on reading and analyzing literature?

It's not difficult to promote personal narrative writing in a literature class. Readers, adolescent or adult, learn from a story by juxtaposing it to the stories of their own lives. Suppose the class is reading *The Catcher in the Rye* and keeping a learning log. Some optional prompts for log entries may be designed to evoke auto-biographical writing. I often follow an idea prompt, which usually produces expressive writing, with a story prompt, which yields a narrative entry. For example:

> (*Idea prompt*) Holden lies a lot. Why?
>
> (*Story prompt*) Tell the story of a time when you felt you *had* to lie.
>
> (*Idea prompt*) Holden learns some things on his journey that bother him pretty badly. What are a couple of them? Why do they trouble him so much?
>
> (*Story prompt*) Tell the story of a time when you learned something that upset you.

A class or small-group discussion, held after students have responded to the idea prompt, seems to promote better realized narratives. Students who opt not to write in response to the idea prompt will often write a story following the discussion.

When it comes time to craft a paper for teacher evaluation, the student has a number of discovery drafts already at hand. I encourage students to share their log entries in small groups, talk about them, and let the group help decide which early draft has the best potential for making a good paper. I accept a certain ratio of narrative to analysis papers, depending on the class or the individual student.

≡Nine

Narrative of Place:
A Grounding in the Senses

*F*ifteen-year-old Carrie, a student in the spring semester of eighth grade, was in love. Day after day she celebrated the fact in her journal in words that recalled Top-40 song lyrics and sentimental greeting cards, invariably ending with the formula, "Our love is 4-ever!" A slower student on an Individual Educational Plan, Carrie didn't want to write about anything else, and in fact had written almost nothing before this; so I accepted the genre and tried tactfully to encourage a few specifics within it. "What does David look like?" I asked. "When you go out together, what do you do for fun? Show me." A few details began creeping into her journal: David had "gorgeos" wavy hair, liked horror films. Then one day I suggested, "Tell me about a particular place where you and David enjoy being together." That night she wrote:

> Yesterday at David's barn we were talking and he was feeding the cows. I said something funny and we laughed hard. Then we sat and the barn got really quiet, the air was still but stinky, and the cows just looked all around. We were sitting at the windowsill by the door and I was looking at the stars when David started to tickle me, I ran from him. He chased me to the end of the barn. There he held me tightly in his arms, he twerled me around and picked me up off the barn floor. Then his Dad came in and David let go of me. We talked and laughed while his Dad milked and the machines slurped away.
>
> *— Carrie, 15*

Carrie grew up in dairy farm country; the cow barn was a setting familiar to her all her life. Somehow, against that friendly, stinky backdrop, that real place, she was able to offer a glimpse of the real Carrie and David and their love for each other. James Britton says, "The most fundamental and universal kind of learning for human beings is learning from experience, which means bringing our past to bear upon our present" (1982, 100). In this case, Carrie was not bringing past *events* to interpret the experience of being in love, which, after all, was new to her, and for which she could previously find no language but the shallow bromides of popular culture. What she did bring out of her past was the concrete *image* of a place familiar to her senses even before she had language to describe it. No doubt the cow barn reverberated, both for her and for David, with early experience and learning; it was an important part of the particular societal background they shared. To Carrie, the barn was safe and solid; there was nothing abstract about it, nothing vaguely conceptual, like the idea of love—nothing but cows, and stars, and slurping machines. The specific, sensory language she mustered to evoke the barn carried over to her narration about herself and David because she and he were a natural part of that setting. In its context, she was able to abandon vacuous sentimental formulas and begin to use story to shape her personal experience of love, "to put its timeless miracles into the particulars of experience, and to locate the experience in time and place" (Bruner 1986, 13). Carrie understood the difference and was pleased with her own achievement; her journal for the rest of the year became a specific, detailed portrait of a very pretty romance.

Place as the Locus of Sensory Memory

Given an autobiographical or a free writing assignment, a significant percentage of my adolescent students choose to write what I have come to call "narrative of place." In each instance the setting is extremely familiar and is or has been the locus of events—often habitual or apparently trivial—that evoked strong emotion, either positive or negative, in the writer, who to some degree reexperiences those emotions and becomes intensely involved in the writing. In every case, the setting is seen as playing an important role in the actions that occurred there. The place may still exist as a backdrop for current events, like the barn in Carrie's piece, or it may exist only in memory, like a warm and welcoming house that was lost when the grandparents decided to move into a condominium. Often, although not always, the writer recalls other people who played an important role within a particular setting. The common thread running through all these pieces, though, is a place like Carrie's barn, familiar from earliest childhood, solid and real, caught in the sensory web of a child's earliest perceptions.

Often an adolescent's first attempt to write about memories of childhood takes the form of a narrative of place. I believe this is true because, unlike the unfolding of significant events, the place—a house, a camp, an attic, or whatever it may be—is a constant in memory. What occurred there may need to be interpreted, but the place itself needs only to be invoked. It looms as a dominant presence in the child's world, unarguably real. "Readers believe that writers able convincingly to reproduce reality can be trusted accurately to say what that reality means" (Hesse 1989, 111). Adolescent writers, making a strong effort to convince themselves as well as their readers of both the reality of their experience and the validity of their interpretation, use the tangible reality of their setting as the touchstone for meaning.

The Learning Involved in Writing a Narrative of Place

In going back to re-create a remembered place in writing, the teenager engages in several valuable learning processes. First, he is dealing with a setting that he has hitherto known only in preconceptual thought. The shapes, smells, sounds, and textures are embedded at the very roots of the writer's experience; they are part of his substance, and his knowledge of them lies deeper than words. Second, he is using written language to re-create symbolically a physical setting, seeking just the right words to convey those vivid sensory impressions. Third, the adolescent writer

brings newly developed conceptual skills to bear on the emotional significance of events that occurred within that setting and thus learns important truths about both himself and the social context within which he developed. Therefore the writer is dealing conceptually with the "unity of perception, speech and action," which Vygotsky finds to be the center of uniquely human (i.e., higher level) forms of behavior (Cole and Scribner 1978, 26).

In some narratives of place, dealing with the emotional content of the events that occurred there amounts almost to an exorcism. This is the case for Andrea in her personal narrative entitled "A Moment of Fear." She describes being alone in her bed on a dark cold night and hearing a noise on the stairs:

> It wasn't like a footstep, nor was it like anything moving towards me, but a sudden creak, as if pressure had been put on a weak spot in the floor, and had not yet been released.
>
> As I open my eyes, I tell myself not to worry — it's only the wind, or a tree brushing the house. It's no use. My mind begins to whirl viciously with all the possible things that could be making the noises; ghosts, goblins, burgulars, monsters, the wicked witch, a slimy creature with fangs and claws and eighteen legs! I am more frightened now than I think I've ever been in my whole life!
>
> "Mommy! Mommy!" I scream frantically, and then I begin to cry. My mother comes in and turns on my light, and all is quiet. Nothing is stirring. I glance around my little room, first at the door, then the window. Everything is at rest in its usual spot; my dresser with my music box, my doll cradle with 'Baby that-a-way' and Teddy, my box of toys, my big bear Bo-Bo, and my pillow. (I love my pillow, and can not go anywhere overnight without it, not even to Grandma's!)
>
> — *Andrea, 14*

Here Andrea consciously structures her experience by juxta-posing the list of imaginary horrors with the list of safe, famil-iar, tangible objects in her room. Her parenthetical comment about the pillow reinforces the depth of reassurance these objects offer her. The actual terror she felt at the time of the event is ten years behind her; she is now able to deal with the dark void of her fears and to understand them as the perceived loss of her safe world and her proper place in it. In this instance, the elements that constitute "place" are symbolic of personal identity.

Narrative Stance: Participant, Spectator, and Evaluator

In his essay "Writing to Learn and Learning to Write," James Britton distinguishes between the participant in an event and the spectator of it. Four-year-old Andrea, hearing the noise, experiencing the fear, and crying out for comfort, is a partici-pant in the event; it is happening *to* her, and the language she uses in responding to her situation ("Mommy! Mommy!") is designed to affect the situation itself, to change the course of it. Andrea ten years later is a spectator at the same event, which now exists only as a representation in her memory. The reason she remembers the incident so well is because it was remarkable; it stood out as an aberration in a secure childhood. She was not able at the time it occurred to reconcile her terrors with her comforts. Britton says, "If an event is too unlike our expecta-tions we have to respond as best we can, because events don't wait for us; but we are left, after it's over, with an undigested event, an undigested experience" (1982, 102-3). The language Andrea uses ten years later to recall her experience, therefore, is consciously interpretive. She employs the precise detail of set-ting as a representation of reality both to validate her author's stance and to banish her imaginary childhood fears. Again in Britton's words, she is, by the act of writing, "Going back over things to come to terms with them — to deal with as yet undi-gested events. . . . to savor feeling *as feeling* in a spectator role" (1982, 104-5, emphasis in original).

The author's stance is an interesting variable in narratives of place. Since one of the chief reasons for reworking a representation of an event is to evaluate it, the writer must make some significant choices about how most effectively to relate the memory to the evaluation. While the setting remains concrete and immediate in all of these narratives of place, the narrator may stand in any relation to that setting and the events that occurred there. The writer more or less deliberately chooses a form that seems appropriate to the purposes of the story.

Carrie's journal entry, designed to capture a moment, is expressive in tone, informal, not far removed from speech. The feeling of joy is evoked by a simple recitation of events still fresh in memory, as yet only lightly shaped by the distancing of representation and organization. Andrea's piece, by contrast, is literary in intent. It follows the conventions of story and uses sophisticated sentence structures; also — although the controlling voice of the rational adolescent comes through in phrases such as "a slimy creature with fangs and claws and eighteen legs!" — the narrative remains within the point of view of the four-year-old. Her evaluation is embedded within the careful structure and emotionally charged language. A third approach may be seen in this excerpt from Shannon's paper, "Secret World," in which she tells of a favorite childhood pastime, exploring her grandmother's attic:

A doorway made of thick cobwebs gathered my full attention, it was so massive. I ran over to it with amazement forgetting about the floors being weak. The cobwebs looked like a fence to me, something for a barrier meaning no trespassing. I was curious to see what was beyond that wall. I touched the webbed fence, EEWH!! my hand stuck to it. Cobwebs hung everywhere off the high rotting beams, I think that's what made it so spooky. I liked it. I liked the fear that was inside of me and excitement that followed it.

— *Shannon, 16*

It's hard to imagine two more different memories of childish fear than Andrea's and Shannon's. Both girls use the setting to define themselves, but Andrea achieves definition through identification with place and Shannon through opposition to it. Also, unlike both Andrea and Carrie, Shannon appears as an evaluative spectator within her own representation of a remembered event, moving freely back and forth between the actions of her exploration as a small child and her commentary on them as an adolescent. Her piece is neither dominantly expressive, like a journal entry, nor purely story. It is a personal narrative essay containing both a narrative stance and explicit argument concerning the nature of her interaction with her setting. The reader already has a sense of this intrepid child who would breach the webbed barrier, but it is a discovery of some complexity for Shannon to realize that "I liked it. I liked the fear that was inside of me and excitement that followed it."

The Role of Metaphor in Narrative of Place

A more subtle and more generalized form of evaluation appears in many narratives of place written by adolescents. This is the metaphor. Immersing themselves in settings that define the boundaries of childhood, young writers find things within those settings that resonate with meaning. Often, in consciously crafted pieces like Andrea's and Shannon's, echoes of children's stories sound in the constructs, and the metaphors familiar from literature are incorporated into real-life settings. The witch and the teddy bear are universal representatives of fear and comfort, respectively, in Andrea's culture; Shannon's attic takes on the feel of the Halloween haunted house, which generations of children have approached, in story or pageant, with a shiver and a sense of adventure. Shaping metaphors within the narrative enhances students' achievements in writing as well as their personal understanding of themselves and the events they describe. The child, the physical setting, the social background, and the event all may be reciprocally illuminated in a single complex symbol.

Shannon's cobweb curtain is this sort of metaphor. It is at the same time a fence, "a barrier meaning no trespassing," and a doorway. Grandmother's attic is thus both a scary world that discourages exploration and a safe place in which to begin breaking down the prohibitions and extending the boundaries of childhood. The cobweb curtain may also be seen as obscuring the gateway to the past, as Shannon delves into old family treasures on the other side and begins opening up what E. J. Hobsbawm calls the "twilight zone between history and memory" (1987, 3). First seen as "massive," an object of fear, the cobweb barrier yields to the child's hand and becomes an invitation to excitement.

Cognitively, Shannon goes far beyond the simple evocation of place with this conscious use of metaphor. For one thing, she has understood how, at an early age, she used her environment — and altered it, tearing away the cobweb curtain — for the purpose of her own growth and knowledge of the world. For another thing, she achieves narrative technique on a high plane; the use of metaphor generalizes her experience and makes it accessible to the reader on multiple levels. In their introduction to Vygotsky's *Mind In Society*, Cole and Scribner assert that "for the adolescent, to recall means to think. Her memory is so 'logicalized' that remembering is reduced to establishing and finding logical relations; recognizing consists in discovering that element which the task indicates has to be found" (1978, 51). In the narrative of place, where natural (sensory) memory of a physical setting intersects with representational memory of an event, the element that has to be found most naturally emerges as metaphor, the enduring symbol of a fleeting occurrence.

Even very early in adolescence, writers of narrative of place find metaphors that show a keen and subtle understanding of their social environment. Tara, thirteen, writing of the city apartment into which she moved at the age of four with her newly divorced mother, describes "an old porch with red paint that was chipped like nail polish that slightly shows the fingernail." In a single sentence she captures the brave front of life in that neighborhood, a brightly cheerful, but poor and somewhat tawdry setting. During the first week of school, eighth grader Kyle sums up a place that has become entirely *too* familiar: "Out of a faucet came the rust of boring summer." These students had not yet learned a definition of metaphor when they produced their narratives, but they understood very well its power to capture the fundamental flavor of the place they were describing.

As an arena for organizing natural and representational memory, establishing relationships through narrative form and metaphor, and achieving tremendous satisfaction in a written product, the narrative of place is a valuable genre for adolescent writers. Because it is amenable to a variety of narrative forms, it allows for success across the spectrum of writing abilities. Often the narrative of place gives my students on Individual Educational Plans, like Carrie, their first experience of pride in a written assignment. In a composition class, I use it to replace the problematic "descriptive essay," which I have always considered an artificial genre. Here, in the narrative of place, description is embedded in and serves the meaning of story, which is the way it is most often found in literature.

Practical Matters

To introduce the narrative of place, I usually lead my students through an exercise in guided imagery. I ask them to place a pen or pencil and a blank sheet of paper on their desks; then, turning off the overhead lights to make the atmosphere in the room soft and natural, I instruct them to find a comfortable position, relax, and close their eyes. Some students may feel more comfortable if they keep their eyes open, looking only at the blank paper in front of them.

Quite slowly, with pauses between sentences, I say something like this:

"You're walking through a meadow in summertime. You're feeling happy and carefree. Look down at the wild flowers. Feel the long soft grass under your feet as you walk. Look up at the sky. Notice your shadow striding along with you.

"Now see that your shadow is growing smaller. Look down at your hand and see that it is small and plump, a child's hand. You've walked back into your childhood. You're very happy; you love this summer day. Run a little. Jump around.

"Now look ahead of you and at the end of the meadow you see a very familiar place. This is a place you loved as a child. It may be a place outdoors. It may be a house, or a particular room in a house. Walk up to this place.

"Slowly, now, enter this place that you loved as a child. Look around. Take your time, look around carefully. See it as clearly as you did then.

"Move around in this place. Touch something familiar, feel it under your hand. Touch something else.

"What do you hear? Are there special sounds that go with this place? Any familiar smell associated with it? Maybe somebody is coming to join you there, someone who shared this space with you—a playmate, or an adult, or a pet.

"What did you like to do in this place?

"When you see this place perfectly clearly, you may begin to write. Describe it so exactly that your reader can see it too."

The majority of responses are lyrical and lovely. A number of students find in this exercise the basis for a narrative of place.

$\equiv Ten$

Expressive Writing, Journals, and Learning Logs

I am the one who sits behind the girl with the long flowing black hair.

As the class goes by my attention is drawn to her. I am not ignoring what the teacher says, by all means, no. I am still listening to the teacher her smooth voice informing me and directing me. But I only look at the girl infront of me.

I focus on her long black [hair] as it lays on her shoulder. I watch her from behind and wonder what she is thinking. I wonder what the expression on her face is.

I know a lot about her, I know who she is and what she does. I'm sure that this knowledge affects the way that I think of her and I wonder what I would think if I didn't know her.

I am the one who is leaning on the desk, his head supported by his left hand.

My head is tilted a bit.

I'm the one who is just staring at the back of the girl infront of me.

It may look like I'm not paying attention to the teacher but really I am. Well, maybe not all the time.

Sometimes I just focus on the flowing black hair of the girl infront of me; where her hair rests on the back of her shoulders.

The sound of the air conditioner seems terribly loud. As loud as a river when you stand next to it. It echos in your ears

Sometimes all I hear is the classroom behind the divider.

—Peter, 17

Let me go not in a physical sense Let me go not in a mental sense in a spatial sense in time and life go well isn't that life what is life? Definition (by computer readout): "Blahhh!" My mind always falls apart when I get to the readout I look at the board it says I don't

want to let go which brings to mind the poem Something there is
that doesn't like a fence I think that's it and then I don't want to
stay here where does that leave me

Only time and space time and space (computer definition): Bah
that computer d*mn

Let me go I want to go sounds like a song go: (computer definition): Computers are useless you can't push buttons for answers
forever I want to let go let go: (Mark definition): Hum this is a tuffy
oh I'll figure this out later later (definition by me) in the future
maybe never

go to sleep. go where? to sleep definition: (that's an easy one) to
bed ("instrument of man")

("another one")

I sleep eight hours every day in the institution institution what's
that institution: this thing man invented invented: action taken by
institution is institution life life: best summed up in the letters a i c
t t a (the best of the best)

          phrase
best: ‹   used by the institutions
          praise

etc.

etc.: something equivalent to a computer readout

—Mark, 13

Each of these two pieces was written at white heat in a full
class setting in response to a teacher prompt. Each was written
near the end of the school year by a fluent, experienced student
writer. The handwritten scripts are sprawling and untidy, most
uncharacteristic of Peter, a meticulous student; Mark's hand-
writing, fair at best, is practically illegible. Both boys seemed
puzzled by what they had done and were a little reluctant at
first to share, even with a trusted teacher, even after months of
open sharing. It was several days before Peter handed in his
journal with the entry intact, and Mark, who liked to push
against the rules, indicated that he thought he had failed to meet
some unspecified requirement.

I often give a brief stimulus, which students are free to use or
ignore, at the start of an in-class journal writing session. I had
asked Peter's group, a junior/senior composition class, to write

in their journals anything that seemed appropriate beginning with the phrase "I am the one who . . . " Many of the students worked a long time on this entry, but Peter—whose writings were almost always complex and careful, couched in a deliberate reasoned prose—finished very quickly. I remember actually being a bit annoyed with him because he sat gazing at Kim's hair for such a long time before getting out his folder and going on to work on something else. He and Kim had dated the year previously, and were soon to begin dating again; the tension between them in the interim appeared in both their journals. The emotional tone of this entry—his words almost caress her hair—is very different from the rational, judgmental tone in which he usually wrote of her.

The stimulus for Mark's class is one of my favorites to use after an atmosphere of trust has been established with younger adolescents. I write on the board and ask the students to respond to these words:

Let me go
I want to let go
I don't want to let go

I don't remember now where this stimulus originated, but it speaks to the young teenager just beginning to feel the pull away from home, family, and adult authority. It has prompted many thoughtful and surprising journal entries, but none more so than Mark's. He was, as one might guess from his writing, a computer whiz. Required to sign up for an "interest group," he had been torn between creative writing and computer but had decided on writing because he already knew everything they were going to learn in the computer group anyway.

The Nature of Expressive Language

These two pieces of writing defy categorizing. They belong to no genre. They are part of that amorphous class of utterance that James Britton calls expressive language. Daily conversation is the prime locus of expressive language, the kind of talk that shares the gossip, gets errands done, and mulls over issues of current interest. It is expressive language that lies closest to actual experience and that captures the emotional flavor of the experience. It emerges at the point where life (action, perception) and language intersect. Like all language, its function is organizational and evaluative; its purpose is to shape an individual and communal response to life's events.

Much expressive language is loosely narrative in structure, but elements of argument, exposition, and analysis are imbedded in the story. Members of a family coming home in the evening tell each other about their day, re-creating the events to validate and judge them, and incorporating into their own version the comments and judgments of the others. So the day is pinned by language into memory and fitted into the great complex of other memories of other days. A friend once told me that the best reason for getting married is to have someone with whom to share the story of your day.

PEANUTS reprinted by permission of UFS, Inc.

Expressive language is spontaneous, not self-conscious. Although used to shape events, the words themselves lack an imposed formal structure. What they show is an individual engaged with the world, making a first attempt to clarify the interaction between herself and her situation. It is because of this sense of engagement that expressive language, both spoken and written, is vitally important for adolescent learners. The teenage writer—*any* writer—who does not have the opportunity to deal with an idea at the point where emotion and language meet will have a very difficult time putting substance into the idea in more formal terms.

Expressive Language in the Classroom

Expressive speech is easy to come by in the classroom; any teacher knows how a focused discussion is likely to wander off into apparent byways of reminiscence, anecdote, and conjecture, the need for which has been made clear by Nancy Martin and other researchers:

> The very features which characterize expressive language—its looseness, its relative inexplicitness, its focus on the speaker's own vision—themselves give access to thinking; any attempt at this stage to divert a speaker from *what* he is saying to *how* he is saying it will be a diversion to his thinking.
>
> Thus, it would seem that expressive language should be seen as the base from which we move into other modes when they are needed, and to which we revert in new or difficult situations. This would mean that teachers of all subjects could rest easy with their pupils' everyday language for much more of the time than most of them now think is appropriate, and they could also encourage it, and create situations where it could occur, knowing its importance to a learner. (Martin 1983, 12, emphasis in original)

Expressive writing is harder than speech to promote, because writing itself is an imposed skill and is therefore less likely to be seen by the student as personally necessary:

> Unlike the teaching of spoken language, into which children grow of their own accord, teaching of written language is based on artificial training. . . . Instead of being founded on the needs of children as they naturally develop and on their own activity, writing is given to them from without, from the teacher's hands. (Vygotsky 1978, 96)

Talk is ephemeral and may be infinitely adjusted, but writing makes a permanent commitment to an utterance. Children learn very early that writing involves not just thought, but a product governed by strict assessable rules. Students who learn to feel the *need* to write—who learn like James Britton that "we write, often, in anticipation and in hope, and when we have written discover what it was we meant to say" (1970, 20)—must find some forum, safe from judgment, for their first tentative, expressive efforts.

The Journal as a Locus for Expressive Writing

The most common forum for expressive writing in high school is the journal. To be effective at all, student journals must have the privilege of privacy. I am the only reader of my students' journals. If writers don't want me to read particular entries, they simply fold the page over, and I don't read them.

Also, the journal must never be evaluated as a product (though students will often ask for evaluative comments on the content of a particular entry). Nature writer Gale Lawrence stresses that at the core of a journal there are "no rules! It's one of the few places left open to the impulse of the creator. Language is, after all, an organic impulse beneath all this apparatus we — English teachers — have imposed to make it communication" (1990). Paradoxically, although many adolescents become journal writers as a result of being required by an English teacher to keep a journal, the point of requiring it is to establish a safe place for written language — possibly risky, outrageous, or painfully self-revealing — where English teachers may not interfere.

I believe that journals are often a valuable learning tool for adolescents, but I believe also that if they are to do much good for the majority of students, they present an enormous responsibility for the teacher. It is always a delicate juggling act to decide when it is all right to ask students to consider particular issues in their journals. It can also be difficult to respond appropriately to very personal entries, but the response is important. By far the greater part of expressive language is immediately communicative; by its nature it seeks a reply. Some adolescents are like Anne Frank in that they have the ability to internalize an audience, but most require feedback. The teacher who hopes for active, inquisitive, self-defining writing in student journals needs to hold up her end of the dialogue. It's time-consuming to do so, but I've found generally that students reward my responsiveness by writing journals that are worth whatever time they require to read them.

I distinguish between journals and what I call learning logs. The content of journal entries is very much up to the individual writer, whereas the learning log provides the student with a forum for personal expressive responses to reading or classroom assignments. Although the form of response is left entirely up to the student, I often make specific assignments—so many pages or an issue to consider—in the learning log. Sometimes students are required to share learning log entries, but the student always has the option not to share journal entries. I don't ask students to keep a journal and a learning log simultaneously, but once they are familiar with both, my students freely mix learning notes with personal entries in either forum.

A class that is keeping journals or learning logs offers the teacher not only responsibility, but also the huge advantage of knowing her students very well indeed. It is a first step in developing a classroom culture that accommodates the differences and accepts the contributions of each member. In a setting where real communication exists between teacher and students, trust and self-confidence build, along with the sense that "I can say what I really think, and what I say is important." Adolescents who are encouraged to use expressive language in both discussion and journal keeping become active, cooperative learners, building on each other's discoveries as well as their own.

Not all expressive language is narrative; much of it is a sort of hybrid genre that weaves a thread of story through passages of opinion and speculation (see chapter 11). Many journal entries, the common sort that tell about and comment upon the events of daily life or re-create bits of memory, are primarily narrative. Even the informal ruminations about literature and discourses about issues in the writer's life tell a story of sorts; at the least they tell of the writer's interaction with someone else's story. I like Joanne Cooper's equation of the *journal* with a narrative *journey* of the self through time and context:

> A notebook, a diary, or a journal is a form of narrative as well as a form of research, a way to tell our own story, a way to learn who we have been, who we are, and who we are becoming. We literally become teachers and researchers in our own lives, empowering ourselves in the process. . . . It is a kind of journey, a journey from one moment to the next, from one entry to the next. . . . Telling our

stories through journal writing becomes a quest for understanding in integration, a bridging of the inner mindscape and the outer landscape. (1991, 99)

Expressive Language and Inner Speech

Some journal entries—Peter's and Mark's, for example—are exciting as pieces of writing because they are so effective in building that bridge between inner and outer. Although expressive, they bear little resemblance to the daily diary type of entry. They seem to be much more private than ordinary expressive language, less aimed at eliciting a response. The condensed language, the lack of ordinary conventions of communication, the speed and intensity of the writing process, all suggest that these are fairly faithful externalizations of inner speech. The writers are engaging not so much with their world as with themselves.

Developmentally, internal speech is considered to have the same roots as expressive language (Vygotsky 1986, 243-44). Both originate in and diverge from egocentric speech—the fragmentary narrative with which small children direct and communicate their play. Expressive language extends the social communicative function, while internal speech—symbolic thought—maintains the directive function (the running narrative that makes sense of life) in a condensed, idiosyncratic language unique to each individual. Twentieth-century authors have sought to represent internal speech by the "stream-of-consciousness" technique.

Artists create original work by communicating their internal visions and symbols in a culturally shared form. I suggest that journal entries like Peter's and Mark's, expressive of internal rather than external events, rise from the same artistic source; they tap into some deep spring where language, feeling, and *thought* are inextricably merged. In this profound personal center, Peter bypasses his acculturated rational stance and discovers that he is "the one who" possesses a more generous and contemplative self. Mark, by contrast, is struggling with the tension between thought and the communication of thought. His piece, which implicitly questions the impersonal authority of "computer definitions," is actually a reflection on the roles different

127

kinds of language play in the acquisition of knowledge.

Expressive language is personal language. Whether we turn it outward as social communication or inward as a symbolic guide to our world, it emanates from and reflects ourselves. When we speak or write expressively, we learn. The more opportunities our students are given to explore the cognitive spiral of language and learning, the more they will grow in their ability to use both. Active writers are capable of surprising themselves with depths of understanding they didn't know were there. Writings like Peter's and Mark's endow the student with new self-awareness. They touch the source of artistic creativity. And they do tell a story: the reader accompanies these boys in a captured fragment of the ongoing narrative of their lives.

Practical Matters

Blue books — flimsy little exam booklets, usually eight to twenty-four pages in length — make good learning logs. They're cheap and lightweight, no mean consideration for a teacher who must provide and periodically haul home class sets of them, and the student may keep a separate one for each book or unit under study. When the class has finished a book or unit, the logs fit easily into the students' classroom folders until it's time to review for exams.

As I mentioned earlier, a writer's journal is different from a learning log in that the keeper of a journal is generating ideas and stories rather than responding to the ideas and stories of other authors. I provide journals for all who want them, but I encourage creative writing and composition students to buy a blank notebook that pleases them. For many of them, the journal becomes a friend, and this is more likely to happen if it has a pretty fabric cover or if the lines on the pages are spaced just right.

I never grade reading logs or journals for the quality of their content, but I do assess quantity. The whole purpose of assigning them is to help students learn to write by writing. Therefore I assign, depending on the class, so many pages a week for a B, more for an A. (Some students will always do less, of course, and they are graded accordingly.) I try to keep from being swamped by taking in logs and journals every other week, each class on a different day; any papers fall due during the alternate week.

≡*Eleven*

Narrative and Argument:
Partnership and Progression

today Daddy went trying to get into the race
but the people said no
so he has to watch *it* on television
I don't know why *that* is
maybe cause there too many people
I think *that* is why why
but he couldn't go in *it*
so he has to watch *it* on television
see on Halloween day then he can run in a race
and I can watch him
see I wish I could watch him
but they said no no no Daddy Daddy Daddy no no no have to
    watch have to have to watch have to watch on television
see on Halloween day
then he can run in a race . . .
tomorrow he'll run run run in the race
he says yes
hooray my mom and dad and a man says you can run in the foot-
    race
and I said *that's* nice of you, I want to
so next week I'm going to run to the foot
and and run in the footrace
cause they said I could
it's nice . . .

— Emily in Narrative from the Crib (Levy 1989, 167)

*T*eachers face a common problem of perception: we
have all gone to college. Long before we started teaching, we

bought into the values of an educational system that requires increasingly abstruse genres of discourse the higher we venture in its ivied halls. As we became more proficient in reading and eventually in writing scholarly papers, we forgot how very specialized these linguistic constructs are—how artificial, in fact, like the dam on a river—a semiotic evidence of the human need to modify nature. And we have probably brought back into the real bare brick world of the high school an expectation that our students' papers will interrupt, control, and utilize the flow of words and ideas instead of gushing along at full spate, with back eddies and sink holes, mud flats and periodic floods. And this is a mistake, because what adolescents need first is encouragement to let their little rivulets of knowledge and thought and language meander, connect, and muster into a powerful stream. Dammed too early, they are at risk of running dry.

Form and Function in the Language of Learning

In academic discourse, as in most models of communication, form follows function. Each genre of scholarly writing—the rigidly objective scientific paper or the carefully structured essay of literary criticism, for example—has evolved its own particular style to encompass specialized branches of esoteric thought. Teachers of adolescents tend to get the relationship backward. Surely, we think, if we teach the correct *form*, the necessary constructs of thought and information will follow somehow, will magically appear inside the proper outlines.

It doesn't work that way. Ideas come first, and they don't come in tidy linguistic packages. Sometimes (and more characteristically to some people) they come as an immediate prompt to action: "Let's see, what'll happen if I try this?" Most often, they come in a messy jumble of words in which the potential for *all* basic forms of discourse—poetry, narrative, and the transactional forms of exposition, argument, analysis—may be tangled up together. Ideas by definition are new to the person entertaining them. They occur because the person needs to learn something; they are fluid in shape, trying on all kinds of word forms, not yet solidified into concept. As we grow older and pursue our interests, we may internalize many of the techniques that carry an idea from its first verbal fumblings to a culturally correct formulation of understanding. But the process of moving from idea to formal conceptual communication is similar for everyone, and it is just that: a process.

The Language of Emerging Ideas

In the monologue quoted in the beginning of this chapter, thirty-two-month-old Emily displays the language of emerging ideas at its most fundamental. Different linguistic experts have various names for this kind of verbalization. Considering Emily's age, Vygotsky would probably call it "egocentric speech," the spoken language by which very young children discover the social rules that govern their lives and shape their play. James Britton might identify it as "expressive language," spontaneous utterance that lies closest to the speaker's thoughts, emotions, and experience. Carol Fleisher Feldman, in her analysis of this particular monologue, calls it "problem-solving narrative" because "it has a tidy and intricate pattern of puzzles posed, considerations raised, and solution achieved" as well as elements that give it "a narrative shape—reported speech of her own and of others, changes of 'voice' from participant to narrator, dialogic patterns, audience replies (*it's nice, hooray*)" (Feldman 1989, 112–13, emphasis in original). No matter what it's called, this is the sort of undifferentiated language—common to all of us from earliest childhood—that first handles the weight of ideas.

Emily's monologue contains the germs of other linguistic forms besides narrative and, in the solution of the puzzle, analysis. There is poetry in the rhythms and repetitions of words. Exposition sets forth a program for the future ("on Halloween day then he can run in a race and I can watch him"); argumentation supports a thesis ("maybe cause there too many people") and makes a judgment ("*that*'s nice of you, I want to"). As she grows older, Emily might use an incident like this to launch herself into a piece of writing; given her precocity with words, it will probably result in a good story, poem, or essay. But chances are that her very first linguistic approach to the event and the ideas it implies will be just as complex a mixture of genres at twelve or twenty as it was at two.

Here, for example, are the musings of a thirteen-year-old, amazingly similar to Emily's in tone, intention, and mix of potential genres:

> Many times I talk to my geese or our dog. And I know why I talk to them, for the simple reason that they listen to me and they don't interupt. They are like a psycietrist. But then I think to myself why don't they talk back to me? Why can't they? Could it be that they can speak in English, but they don't want to speak in English when people are around because they don't want people to know? And many times I'll try and sneak up on our geese and see if they speak when they don't think any people are around them. Always they don't speak, but how I wish that one day my dog would come up and say "Hi, Jeff,". But then I realize that she never will be able to. And then I think backwards what if each and every Animal thought that their type ruled the earth and that everything else is stupid or can't think, like us people think we rule the world or do we rule the world? Or do we think?
>
> *—Jeff, 13*

What a treasure chest of possibilities Jeff has assembled! I can imagine a poem, or maybe a children's story, "The Day the Geese Talked Back." Or a personal essay, "Learning from the Animals," or an argumentative essay, "Rulers of the Earth"— the potential is tremendous. As it happened, Jeff was satisfied with this bit of writing just the way it came out and went on to consider other issues with a more disciplined result—and that's fine, too. There's no reason why a teenager's exploratory writing should have to take on a shape any more defined than that of the daydream floating between his eyes and the blackboard.

The Process of Fitting Idea to Genre

It interests me that the great writing teachers of this generation simply don't make any effort to dictate what form the writer should choose in order to shape an idea. Ken Macrorie, an early proponent of what we have come to know as process writing, makes no reference at all to genre when he identifies the characteristics of *good writing*: it is "clear, vigorous, honest, alive, sensuous, appropriate, unsentimental, rhythmic, without pretension, fresh, metaphorical, evocative in sound, economical, authoritative, surprising, memorable and light" (1984, 29). To illustrate these qualities, he quotes a poem, an advertisement, a sports article, a cookbook, a college teacher's dittoed instruction sheet, and a Sears catalog. His range of everyday examples serves to remind the reader that the academic essay is only one form of communication among myriad possibilities, and a very specialized form at that.

Peter Elbow, in his practical book *Writing Without Teachers*, urges writers in the early stages to try different forms in response to an idea: "Allow your writing to fall into poetry and then back into prose; from informal to formal; from personal to impersonal; first-person to third-person; fiction, nonfiction; empirical, *a priori*. . . . Each way of writing will bring out different aspects of the material" (1973, 54–55). And Donald Murray specifically instructs the writing student, "At this stage of the writing process, when we are still circling the raw material, it's helpful to use genre as a lens. Poets keep seeing poems, novelists stories, reporters news. We can train ourselves to look at the material to see it in terms of different genres" (1984, 75). Murray also advises keeping the needs of the reader, as well as those of the writer, in mind when choosing a genre. "In writing we try to deliver information to the reader that the reader needs or wants. If we look through the raw material and find such information we may have a way of writing the piece" (81).

These teachers understand and utilize two basic concepts in approaching the task of writing:

- Content (idea, raw material) precedes form.
- The writer must go through a *process* of fitting words to ideas and ideas to words, back and forth, until they are congruent. Each modifies, deepens, and clarifies the other.

Writing Instruction and the Crisis in American Education

Writing is a use of language, and we know that development in language and learning is recursive; growth in one is accompanied by growth in the other. Turn that proposition around — lack of growth in one is accompanied by lack of growth in the other — and we begin to see one reason for the current perceived crisis in American education. (There are, of course, many others, which I do not presume to address.)

Pick up virtually any newspaper or magazine and you will find an article having to do with the problem of poor writing skills in our society today. Here, for example, awaiting a trip to the recycler, is *The Montreal Gazette*, September 8, 1992: "University students failing writing tests," leaps from the front page. The problem exists not just in academe but in the workplace as well: "Survey: Workers need better communication skills," states a headline in *The Burlington Free Press* a few days later. The article notes that the 402 companies interviewed "identified writing as the most valued skill but said 80 percent of their employees at all levels need to improve" (Henry 1992, 5A). Even in the educational community, many teachers are themselves diffident writers, and many also are reluctant to judge student writing on any basis other than the inclusion of assigned content. In other words, they are teaching as they were taught: not to write, per se, but only to graft a particular formal style onto the material of their own particular discipline.

I believe that this crisis exists because of a common misperception by curriculum designers and teachers alike about the relationship between writing and learning. Educators trained in the college setting too often fail to realize that *writing to learn* is a necessary step that precedes *writing to communicate what has been learned* (Young 1986, 11). Furthermore, the fact that abstraction and generalization become developmentally possible for adolescents does not mean that they will prefer to choose transactional forms of writing to explore new ideas. Adolescents are, like all of us, most likely to express their learning of any given idea first in nongeneric expressive language like Emily's and Jeff's. Subsequently, if they wish to shape their ideas further, they will probably turn to narrative, for the simple reason that narrative is intuitive and familiar. Wise teachers recognize these natural steps. It is in their best interest and that of their students to encourage and accept nongeneric exploratory writing; to welcome narrative as a valid expression of comprehension; and to help students build bridges between the personal, particular insights of story and the more abstract, general formulations of transactional writing.

Writing to Develop Thinking

Besides lack of familiarity with transactional forms, adolescents face another problem in learning to produce scholarly writing. An academic writer is like a sculptor who starts with a big chunk of knowledge and chips away all that is not essential to his central idea of it. A teenager has trouble doing this because, in most areas, he doesn't yet possess big chunks of knowledge. This is not a fault; he simply hasn't lived long enough to acquire much more than bits and pieces. Therefore the adolescent writer, especially one in the early years, is more like a muralist whose work grows in size and scope as he finds one idea leading to another. Because teachers want to promote in their students the growth of ideas, information, and the interconnectedness of knowledge, it makes sense for them to encourage writing genres that also promote such growth.

When adolescents feel welcome to produce speculative pieces of writing like Jeff's, especially in the context of a supportive classroom culture, they generate more ideas, write more effectively, and develop more confidence as writers than they do when simply required to turn in a finished product. They learn to think of writing primarily as a technique for empowering their own learning and less as an instrument for teacher assessment, one that can never be played perfectly enough. They involve themselves as learners and take pride in their finished writing because they have invested themselves in its production; it represents their own best thinking. As Peter Elbow says,

Much of the writing we are asked to do in school or work involves explaining someone else's thinking. To do this well we must get inside that other person's idea. . . . When we have to write about the thinking of others, we are especially likely to slip into the path of least resistance, the energy-efficient method: we summarize the ideas without really being there. That's why children who are never asked in school to write about their own thinking often get worse and worse at experiencing thought. (1973, 341)

From Exploratory to Transactional Writing

The path from exploratory or expressive writing to successful transactional writing seems fairly clear. It has been described and documented by numerous authors, including some I have quoted in this chapter. In expressive writing, the writer lays out a palette of possibilities, cycles among forms and between experience and conjecture, gathers a wide range of ideas, begins to develop a focus. I enjoy laying my students' learning logs next to their finished papers; often the anecdotes, struggles for connection, and intuitive leaps in one foreshadow successful argument in the other.

In her learning log on *The Merchant of Venice*, Melissa became caught up in the conflicts among the male characters and made only cursory notes on the character of Portia until she reached Act III, Scene 4. She had noted with disapproval that Portia was in a "pretty dreary situation—she might end up marrying one of those guys she doesn't like," and with approval, "Women in this play very strong—this is *neat!*" But it wasn't until Portia prepared to go to Venice that Melissa suddenly saw her in a rushing wave of insights that combine narrative summary, powerful poetic rhythms, analysis, argument, and prediction:

Portia—'whose souls do bear an equal yoke of love'—love is a burden, a yoke??

Portia is very sensible—'this comes too near to praising of myself', modesty—changes the subject to more practical matters—doesn't let herself get too sentimental or romantic (Bass[anio] chose correct chest, restrained herself) always restraining her feelings!

You really see Portia's character when she is just with Nerissa—she is like a whole different person—like a young girl

Portia is very headstrong and courageous—how many other women of this time would have stolen away to Venice disguised as young men to see their lovers?? What does she have up her sleeve?

Again—she is like a young girl—I will be more like a young man than you, etc.—so different from the somber woman she seems to be around the others—then she is a *lady* and in charge of her *estate*, strong, even a little cold sometimes!

—*Melissa, 16*

This rush of exploratory writing led Melissa directly to a topic and the first hint of a thesis. Here are the first two paragraphs of the fine character analysis she subsequently wrote about Portia. She has refined these ideas and worked in others that arose in her reading of the final two acts. In the last sentence of the first paragraph, she makes explicit the connection between Portia's apparently contradictory character and her position in a society in which women are dominated by men, a connection she goes on to examine. Melissa has also adopted, at a level appropriate for a high school junior, the formal language of literary analysis:

Portia in Shakespeare's "The Merchant of Venice" often comes across as being a woman who is composed and stately, somewhat cold, and forever in control of her feelings. This is not the true character of Portia, however, but rather a front she upholds in a dignified and proud defense of her personage. Although Portia's love and very life is bound by the will of her father, she will not permit anyone to think of her merely as chattel to be won by a riddle.

The true character of Portia is one of a woman who loves deeply; a woman who is much more full of warmth and spirited humor than she often shows. There are moments in the play, such as when she is alone with Nerissa, and when Bassanio chooses the correct casket, when her true soul and character shine through, and the cold politeness and formality can be seen as being only a front.

—*Melissa, 16*

Narrative in Relation to Other Genres

Many English teachers can point to examples of their own students' work that, like Melissa's, illustrate the clear relationship between speculative expressive writing and essay. But this is at heart a book about narrative learning—and there seems to be, alas, no similar *direct* path from good narrative to good transactional writing. As the chapters have rolled by I've kept hoping to find one, but no such luck. The path implied by Macrorie, Elbow, and Murray leads from good thinking processes, coupled and inextricably interwoven with good exploratory writing processes, to good writing in *any* genre. The sticking point for adolescents lies in the fact that the "good thinking process" involved in structuring a transactional paper requires them to work at a new, still developing cognitive level. Adolescents writing a school essay are working almost entirely at the outer limits of their conceptual capabilities, in what Vygotsky calls the "proximal zone of learning" (1978, 187), because they are grappling to fit into their map of reality both the new material itself and the culturally sanctioned way to shape and present it.

It is not the ideas, the content, or the process that distinguish the production of narrative from that of essay. *The only real difference is the way in which the writer organizes the material.* Narrative is structured by chronological relationships, transactional writing by logical relationships. Narrative builds upon concrete particularities, transactional writing upon generalized ideas. That's the entire difference.

Furthermore, each genre even at its purest dips deeply into the other's well. Narrative must contain elements of argument and analysis in order to establish purpose; essay needs narrative anecdotes, examples, and illustrations in order to gain specificity (Dixon & Stratta 1986, 84).[1] A good story must contain conflict. Whether this takes the form of a dialogue between characters or a choice between courses of action, argumentation is crucial to the narrative: "Questions, problems, hypotheses and explanations are the tools of argumentative discourse, but . . . they are put to service in the narrative discourse; they are part

---

[1] I particularly recommend *Writing Narrative–and Beyond* by Dixon and Stratta for its excellent discussion of the interrelatedness of genres and of the gradual emergence of generalization and argumentation in adolescent writing.

of the structure of the story" (Fox 1989, 35). A good essay, by the same token, must tie its generalities to specific examples:

> Effective writing is almost always a story, and we all love to read a story to find how it comes out. Even written arguments, expository essays, and analytical pieces have an imbedded narrative that keeps the reader moving forward.... The most provocative intellectual essays are built on an imbedded narrative. (Murray 1984, 222–23)

Given the shared foundations of all good writing, not to mention the interdependence of narrative and argument, it would seem likely — and it has certainly been my experience — that confident, active adolescent narrators will mature into writers of effective essays. But the growth of analytical thinking is not like the growth of beard or breasts; it is a process of change as much social as organic. It is arguably the most important job of the teacher of adolescents to facilitate the transition. And in my opinion, one of the best ways a teacher can help a student become a good transactional writer is first to help that student become a good *writer*.

Practical Matters

A teacher can leave a lot of lesson planning up to the class, once it has become a community of active writers. One of my favorite plans for a literature class is simplicity itself.

After a reading assignment, I tell my class they're going to do my job for me. It is the responsibility of each student to develop two or three topics, having to do with the reading, that will make good prompts for learning log entries. These topics may be designed to elicit a particular genre (usually narrative) or they may be open-ended. In small groups, classmates discuss their prompts and refine the wording. Each group chooses one or two to present to the full class, and these are written on the board; each student then chooses one of the topics for a log entry.

This lesson is extremely effective in a class accustomed to engaging issues in literature through their own writing. Students usually come up with most of the topics and issues I might have presented, plus a few that had not occurred to me. There are three distinct advantages to having the students generate the assignment: first, as a team they take ownership of the story under discussion; second, they develop a broader and more subtle understanding of the issues through forging the wordings for their prompts; third, they have a wide selection of their own ideas to consider in their writing.

≡Twelve

Stalking the Essay: Transitional, Interdisciplinary, and Hybrid Genres

An art gallery in which all the pictures were mirrors would be boring, and so would a world with only one reflection of existence. There is not simply one objective world, one fixed ground with adequate representations of it in mind; there are multiple worlds in an ecology of multiple biomes and organisms, each constituting cognitive domains of fascinating richness. Those who can live with ambiguity, complexity, and infinite variety can rejoice that there are windows to different worlds in the cognition of an antibody, a bee, a dolphin, a bird, a human, an elemental, or an angel. (Thompson 1989, 120)

Every year, I teach some adolescents—a handful of ninth and tenth graders, a score or more of upperclassmen—who embrace the essay with an eager "Ah ha!" Their minds are maturing; most of them are successful students who have worked as hard to develop their thinking as the school soccer star to develop his legs. The genre makes sense to them because their thought processes already include significant elements of classification, generalization, analysis, and synthesis.

Demystifying the Essay

Most students come to the form with much more difficulty. Many have already had bad experiences with papers or essay exams in which they saw themselves as failures. I have known fluent, enthusiastic story writers to close down and lock in the face of an essay assignment. For these students I do two things at the start. First, I try to demystify the term *essay* by referring to its linguistic origin in the French verb *essayer*, to attempt or try. I tell them that there's nothing absolute about what's said in an essay, or how it's said. It's just a trial, an effort to establish and fix in words the place where they now stand in relation to a body of knowledge, an event, or an issue. "It doesn't hurt to *try*!"

Second, I flood them with models to read until some of them grumble that they thought this was a *writing* class! But what David Huddle says is so clearly true as to seem obvious: "Writers learn the craft of writing by reading the work of other writers" (1991, 77). If there's a convenient, universally applicable canon of model essays somewhere, I have yet to find it. My own file contains not only textbooks and published pieces gathered over the years, but some of my own essays and many of my former students'. Because so many essays are topical, often those written within the local school setting make the most effective examples.

There are several ways English teachers can help their students maintain self-confidence and involvement as they develop into competent essay writers. (If students don't maintain self-confidence and involvement, chances are good that they won't develop into competent essay writers.) One way is to work systematically through nonfiction genres, starting with personal narrative, moving on to transitional genres such as the process paper, character sketch, interview, and/or definition essay, and culminating with the more formally structured essays of exposition, argument, and analysis. This traditional route is the one I follow with tenth- through twelfth-grade composition students—with some very important caveats.

Not all—probably fewer than half—of high school upperclassmen will be able to achieve a complete transition to good transactional writing, considering "survey data which suggests that up to 50 percent of first-year college students are not yet functioning at the formal operational level" (Brooke 1991, 59). And those are just the students who are academically successful enough to go to college. It's pretty disheartening for a teacher to teach a skill at which more than half the class is likely to fail, especially when it is seen as a vital life skill, such as writing effectively. And if it's hard on the teacher, think of what the students are feeling. Many students, hearing the teacher's emphasis on transactional *forms*, spend their effort trying to shape a paper by alien rules instead of trying to communicate well something of importance to them. And too many teachers, given the curricular imperative to teach forms, sigh over their failures and then reward the authors of those awful, empty papers "because they tried."

When I introduce a form, therefore, I try to present it as a tool that may be used to achieve good writing, not as a goal in itself. At the same time, I try to make it clear that my most important goal for the class is to have every student write as well as he can on whatever topics interest him most. With this shift in emphasis, there is also a shift away from the teacher-centered class toward a writing workshop. Students write less to meet the demands of the teacher, more for themselves and each other. They use the formal tools at whatever level they can to say most effectively what's on their mind. Many never progress much beyond transitional forms, but virtually all produce effective pieces of writing that they are proud of.[1]

Peer Interaction and Personal Narrative

The single most important stage of the journey towards more formal writing comes right at the start for my composition students. During the early weeks they develop among themselves a strong support network through the writing, discussion, and positive sharing of autobiographical narratives (see chapter 8). This step takes time, and it can't be rushed; but it's worth it. First, it gives students a kind of flexibility and openness to change in a secure setting:

> Learning in groups . . . is often more effective than learning individually because learning involves more than simply acquiring new

---

[1] I found very helpful Robert E. Brooke's *Writing and Sense of Self*, an NCTE book that describes in detail how and why one teacher of college freshmen made the change from a developmental program based on Piaget's theories to a writing workshop.

> information. It also involves the acceptance of new habits, values, beliefs, and ways of talking about things. To learn is to change: learning implies a shift in social standing — a transition from one status and identity to another and a reorientation of social allegiances. (Trimbur 1985, 90)

Consequently, when the class has become a workshop of people who really care about each other's work, the risky move into new forms becomes a shared adventure, less frightening and more easily achieved than a lonely foray. Also, when adolescents know they are writing for a knowledgeable, interested audience of peers, they make a great effort to write well.

The personal narrative, even though its primary purpose is to tell the author's story, is still an effective transitional genre. Older adolescents quickly understand the concept of narrative stance. They are able to see, in a successful piece of autobiographical writing, that the narrator's choices of detail and emphasis work together to make some point about the event described. Therefore, from the earliest conferences, they are looking in their own and in each other's writing for a central theme (with the understanding that theme includes a stance, one arguable point of view) and for selection of material that supports this theme. It is not so hard, later on, to shift from theme to thesis. Point of view is one of several aspects of narrative that a fluent storyteller can carry over into more formal discourse.

Transitional Genres

The Process Paper The process paper tells the reader, step by step, how to do something. It is a unique genre in that the overall structure is narrative and chronological, but each step must be a model of clear exposition. Most of my students enjoy writing process papers because they have the opportunity to communicate to others something they do well. The most successful papers convey both clear directions for how to carry through an activity and the satisfaction that results. One of my favorite process papers described in delicious detail how to make brownies; it was so well done that the author had to bring in a batch so his classmates could judge his procedures for themselves.

The process paper is a wonderful medium for reenactment. As one student reads his paper aloud, another attempts to complete each step as described. Often the results are funny: I remember a peanut-butter sandwich that consisted of an open jar of peanut butter, spreader inserted, between two slices of bread. Sometimes they are very successful: one of my students, using words alone, taught a well-coordinated classmate to juggle in less than half a period.

The Character Sketch The character sketch, with or without interview, is an ideal transitional genre that includes strong elements of both narrative and essay. The author naturally tells stories specific to the subject and equally naturally relates attributes of the individual to generalized social norms (Dixon & Stratta 1986, 50–60). When my literature students write non-narrative papers, I encourage them to begin with character analysis, like Melissa's essay on Portia (see chapter 11). The student who has read imaginatively enough to bring a character to life will be able in her paper to treat that character like a real person, one whose actions can be both summarized in narrative and evaluated in two cultural contexts—that of the character and that of the analyst.

Teenagers find it fascinating to observe and interview people they know, particularly their parents and grandparents. Such a project connects adolescents with their heritage and helps them bring very familiar people into a new context. It focuses their attention sharply on cultural continuity and change. Several students have commented in their evaluations that during the process of preparing a paper on a parent or older relative they developed a new, more adult relationship with the interviewee. Adolescents become deeply involved in such a project; they feel a strong obligation to present their human subject effectively. They also hardly notice the shift in their own writing from pure narrative to a form that combines the subject's stories with their judgments about the subject.

Often the character sketch/interview represents a kind of breakthrough for a student writer. When Joy entered composition class as a senior, she had serious doubts about her writing. Her skills and confidence grew rapidly as she wrote and engaged in conferences with classmates and with me in a workshop setting. In this excerpt from a charming essay about her mother's child-rearing practices, written as a final exam, Joy moves the reader deftly through family generations and a complex linguistic mix of exposition, narrative, and opinion:

> The way my mother disciplines is modeled after my great grand-mother. She told me a story. One day my great uncles got into this obnoxious habit of sticking their tongues out at each other and it was a little to often. So my great grandmother made them sit down across from each other and stick their tongues out for an hour. It doesn't sound fun to me. Needless to say they still have to stick their tongues out at each other and it's been what, sixty years.
>
> The way it was when she was growing up has a lot to do with the way the society was. You did what was right and that was final. "Kids back then never asked why, they never questioned, they just did." I asked if kids ever wondered in there own mind, why. She said that the way of thinking back then was different and that she can't remember ever wondering, why anything. She thinks, "It was probably easier for kids back then. Less confusion and less complex-ity of everything."
>
> —*Joy, 18*

The Definition Essay A less reliably successful transitional genre than the process paper or the character sketch/interview is the definition essay. I like and use it because the formal require-ments are extremely flexible. Invariably someone, often one of the less academically inclined students, takes advantage of the assignment's open nature to come up with a stunning piece of prose. To prepare, students brainstorm a list of abstract terms for which everyone has a personal, often concrete definition: *freedom, competition, happiness, wealth, beauty,* and so on. This is followed by some exploratory writing and sharing. Often I ask them next to write a poem, using the word they have defined as the title. This isn't always easy ("What? A POEM!? I can't write poetry!"). My intention is to encourage the writers to

explore ideas by experimenting with different genres. Sometimes, having successfully shaped their material through the lens
of poetry, authors will feel satisfied and choose to stop there.

Turning to essay, the writers have the option to be as general
or as specific as they like in the treatment of their chosen topic.
Some students write personal narratives of events that they feel
exemplify the abstract quality; some write the definition as a
thesis and construct a paper citing reasons and examples. Always,
some of these essays are disappointingly bland and clichéd while
others resonate with insight. The act of exploring an emotionally
rich word such as *freedom, happiness, loneliness*, can tap the pure
profound depths of adolescent feeling. And every year, one or two
definitions reduce to ash the paper they're written on. Jason, a
repeating ninth grader placed in composition class more or less as
a last resort, had completed only a few writing assignments in his
high school career before turning in his paper. The classmate who
had become Jason's chief advocate and editor watched with interest as I first read it to see my response:

Hate and the devil

Hate is something out of the black side of the mortal being. It has
power over all the controls and wants of the person that it's in. It is
like a black thunder cloud with the lightning shooting out of it. It is
like the face of the devil with fire spurting out of its mouth and fire
red eyes he talks in a snake voice.

You fall into his grasp till you fill up with rage, till you just can't
stand it any more. By that time he has you where he wants you. "It
is just minutes" he says" before I can have fun with this mortal! It's
just minutes before I can claim more souls."

The mortal tries to fight it off but he just does not have the
strength to do it. He just blows up into a rage. Then by the time he
realizes what he just did it could be too late.

The mortal may not even know what he said or did. He may not
understand why he blew, but he is not to blame for it most of the
time. The devil is just waiting for a weak point in the mortal's self
esteam. He is like a little kid jumping up and down with rambunc-
tions feet waiting to feed on the hate.

—Jason, 15

The first reasonable response to such a paper is not, "What a pity it doesn't follow the rules of genre." It is not even, "Why on earth isn't this boy succeeding in school?" although that follows hard after. It is something to the effect of, "Whoa, that's good writing!"

Developing Writing Skills Across Disciplines

The composition class offers the English teacher a reasonable framework within which to expose older adolescents to the kinds of communication best served by transactional writing. For younger students, and for those following a more general English curriculum, the teacher is wise to collaborate on assignments with a colleague or colleagues in other disciplines. Many middle and junior high schools have shifted to an interdisciplinary model with the goal of integrating the learning and experience of early adolescents. Among other benefits, this model leads to writing across the curriculum—an ideal that is much harder to realize in a traditional model based on separate content areas. In the last few years, I have worked with social studies and science teachers to develop interdisciplinary thematic units for our heterogeneously grouped ninth-grade students; as a consequence, I have made three important and widely applicable discoveries about how to facilitate the transition from writing primarily narrative to writing essay.

First, I found that it makes a lot of sense for younger adolescents to begin their career as transactional writers in the content area disciplines. In science or social studies, students are given both a chunk of knowledge and a textbook model—not very exciting, perhaps, but well structured—to use in shaping it. This doesn't happen in English. Literature does *not* model literary criticism. In asking students to write about literature, we ask them not only to abstract general ideas from a specific narrative, but to present them in a completely different form: double jeopardy. Furthermore, it is difficult to find examples of literary critical analysis that are accessible or interesting to a ninth or tenth grader; those that they do find and use, such as the Cliff

Notes, are so didactic that they close down rather than open up students' ideas about the literature itself.

Instead of asking my ninth graders to write transactional papers in the context of English class, therefore, I offered my services as resident writing expert to the content area teachers. Our students worked on their papers in at least two classes, with at least two teachers taking a serious interest in the processes and outcomes. As a result, the students took the papers seriously also. The science and social studies teachers observed that these papers were deeper in content and better crafted than those they had received in the past.

The Educational Power of Hybrid Genres

Note that I said "at least two teachers." So pleased were we with these small papers that we asked our students at the end of their second thematic unit, the voyage of Columbus, to write a large paper incorporating their learning in all three disciplines. What we assigned was essentially a hybrid genre. My second discovery was the educational power of such a project. The students, who had been writing personal narrative in English ("a voyage into your own past"), assumed the persona of a sailor on one of Columbus's ships. They were to write in first person the story of an event in that sailor's journey, including accurate historical and scientific material.

These ninth graders had in place as they undertook the assignment a wide background of knowledge upon which to draw. They had been reading, watching films, and discussing Columbus's journey from three points of view in three classes a day for a month. Not one freshman failed to turn in a paper — and we had students for whom that was a notable first. Rich in ideas and material, the stories were successful both as communication and as a basis for assessment of learning. Our students went beyond the assignment, combing the library to discover such details as what day of the week Columbus set sail and what kinds of birds might have signalled land. And in its re-creation, they experienced some of the triumphs, misgivings, and cruelties of that bold journey. Rachel, for example, draws in the reader with mood and sensory detail as she leads up to the first sighting of land:

> I stand on board the Nina, gazing up at the moon, which is lighting up the deck of the ship. It is making it look eerie, but beautiful. I can hear the waves slapping gently against the side of the boat. I am very homesick. I miss my family and I pine for the sight of land. I don't know if I'll ever get home. That really scares me.....
>
> I am watching the Pinta scudding through the water to starboard of our ship. It is a very quick ship compared to ours and the flagship, the Santa Maria. Sometimes I wonder what it's like to be on that ship, If they're as nasty as the sailors on my ship.....
>
> Two days ago, Columbus, the admiral of the fleet, thought he sighted land. Other people did, too. We chased what we saw until it disappeared this morning. I was so disapointed, and my heart sank like a boulder. Now we're still searching the horizon and only seeing the orange sunset when the day ends...
>
> — *Rachel, 14*

Integrative Thinking and the Hybrid Genre

My third discovery about the teaching of writing in an interdisciplinary setting was originally made and shared with me by a colleague. Science teacher Larry Brewer, interested by the willingness of his students to write in a hybrid genre about their learning, deliberately left the choice of form up to them when he assigned a paper on historical geology: "Follow a grain of sand through the various transformations it might undergo throughout its existence. Describe how rocks are formed, transformed, moved and broken down through erosion and weathering."

The papers that he received were longer and more detailed than he expected, and they came in a variety of genres. Comparing the response of these students to others he had taught in more conventional ways for more than twenty years, he said,

> I think their understanding of the material is probably as good if not better, but they're more excited about learning. They're being more creative about relating material to what they've learned earlier and incorporating material from their other classes. Something has happened to allow them to feel the freedom to do what they want to

151

do; the assignment could be dry, but they elected to be really creative. (Brewer 1992)

In reading these papers, I found that a number of students went far beyond a simple retelling of geological processes (or a comic odyssey of one grain of sand) to open up serious philosophical questions. In the past Larry had restricted his young students to a "correct" standard form of scientific writing, thereby limiting their potential to pose questions and draw connections with other areas of knowledge as part of the writing process. This time, leaving the door open for exploration, he found more than scientific fact in their papers. Guin, for example, makes effective use of narrative form as a vehicle both for communicating scientific knowledge and for probing its implications. For five pages her "Life of George Silicate" contains an accurate recounting of geological transformations within the framework of a funny story. At the end, however, when George is expelled by an eruption from Mt. St. Helen's, the narrator is moved to speculate about the power and interdependency of natural phenomena:

> After the initial excitement had worn off and we had cooled off I looked around. I could see nothing above us, but there were trees down for at least 25 kilometers. There was at least 2-5 centimeters of ash covering everything, in some areas there was mud and landslides that were over 180 meters deep. I couldn't believe my eyes, how was it possible that some melted rock with gas could be so devastating to the earth it touched. We minerals are usually such peaceful things, if you had asked me if I thought that I would kill many living things when i was flying through the air having the time of my life I would have said you were crazy. Now I know that nothing is as it appears and everything is capable of plundering devastation on something else.
>
> *—Guin, 14*

The experiences of my ninth graders have convinced me that an interdisciplinary thematic approach fosters cognitive growth and excitement about learning for students and teachers alike. We have become a learning community, each contributing what we can to help build the group's expanding framework of knowledge and ideas. I speak as a convert; at the beginning, although I held my peace in front of colleagues and classes, I had some reservations about the educational value of tossing teachers, students, and disciplines into a common thematic pot. Having long been involved in English curriculum development, I had become too attached to a clear, discipline-based curricular framework. As a writing teacher — even with my commitment to a workshop format — I worried that my students would no longer be progressing along an orderly continuum of skills.

In fact, we did muddy up those tidy guidelines quite a bit. But it seems that for each failure to produce a defined sequential outcome, we generated a whole cluster of new learning processes. By now I am very enthusiastic about the *inter*disciplined (as opposed to *un*disciplined) sprawl of interests and pursuits among our freshmen. If they write in hybrid genres, it is a natural response to the fact that they are learning hybrid disciplines. In their papers, as in their classes, knowledge spills over from one content area to enrich another. No science journal would publish "The Life of George Silicate," but in very few science journals do humor, personal involvement, and a thoughtful consideration of human consequences shine from the pages. Should Guin, already a good *writer*, choose to become a scientist, she will readily learn to write the proper objective and impersonal genre. She will also continue, to the benefit of the scientific and cultural community, to appreciate the "ambiguity, complexity, and infinite variety" of the world she writes about.

Practical Matters

Many younger adolescents are capable of learning basic research skills before they are ready successfully to organize an extended expository or thesis paper. My colleagues in the content areas and I often assign a biographical paper, which has proved to be a successful hybrid genre for a number of our ninth-grade students. They follow all the appropriate research processes: locating and documenting sources of information, taking notes, summarizing and paraphrasing, using parenthetical citations. The only difference lies in the organization of the paper. There is no need to structure the essay by idea or attribute, since the story of someone's life may best be told chronologically. However, like the interview or character analysis, a biographical essay invites judgments, both the author's own and those that appear in the source material; as a result, analysis and argument develop organically within the narrative context. Students who know that judgment and opinion are important requirements are also less likely to turn in deadly paraphrases of the encyclopedia.

☰ Thirteen

The Teacher as Oracle

As characters in the classroom drama, all of us read each other. (Pagano 1991, 199)

Teaching has provided the answers to much speculation about the real nature of people. There are no duplicates of individuals anywhere in the world, which is indeed vast, and each one is miraculously unique. To winkle out that uniqueness has been a perpetual task in my job, and in doing it I have found ample cause for confidence in people. Perhaps teaching is about seeing behind this one's obscenities and that one's silence. (Rosen 1988, 9)

The reader who has come this far must share with me an interest in the value of narrative in adolescent learning. In this final chapter I want to move away from generalized theory and examples to explore my own specific educational beliefs and their implications for classroom practice. The beliefs I consider to be at least potentially empowering for any teacher; how they are implemented will vary according to each one's needs. My personal techniques for teaching effectively may work for others, or they may not. Teachers, fortunately, differ from each other as much as their students do; there are many effective ways to do the right thing.

The Wisdom of Learning Styles Theory

I believe that no single teaching or learning technique works for all students. This may sound like a truism, but it's amazing how many teachers—particularly those working with adolescents—try to teach all their students the same content at the same time in the same way. When my son was in fifth grade, I visited his team-taught class and watched Mrs. Kelly, one of the finest teachers I have ever met, explain to a select "advanced" arithmetic group how to divide mixed numbers. It was an excellent lesson. Mrs. Kelly spoke in clear terms with good examples, addressing her young charges with friendly respect. I was so impressed by her technique that for a while I followed along, but eventually I glanced at my son.

He was drawing a picture.

Of course, he already knew how to divide mixed numbers; he was forestalling boredom in one of many ways he developed throughout his years of schooling. Looking at the group as a whole, I saw six kids who were intent on the lesson. Four more were in and out, and five were paying little or no attention. And yet this was a good lesson, beautifully delivered to a group judged to be ready for it. It was one of the most important lessons *I* ever learned.

There is a great deal of material on learning styles and temperament now available to teachers. In terms of classroom management, nothing has been more helpful to me. My own favorite resource is a book entitled *Please Understand Me* based on the Myers-Briggs Type Indicator (Keirsey and Bates 1984). Mrs. Kelly taught me that at any one moment different students have different needs; this book taught me to understand, accept, and begin to deal with the differences. An example: some of our students are process-oriented; for them, the purpose of doing something is to *do* it, and they have little interest in the results. Others are product-oriented; their reason for doing something is to achieve some worthwhile outcome, a paper, drawing, performance, and so on that they can be proud of. Another example: some students like rules and want to do things *right*; others question rules and want to do things in a *new way*.

A study of temperaments and learning styles also helped me define my own working preferences. Teachers are as likely as any other human group to compare themselves judgmentally with their peers, scornful of some whose approach differs from theirs, but anxious at the same time that they might themselves be found lacking. Learning theory helped me become secure enough to acknowledge the inherent strengths and weaknesses of my own teaching. I am subsequently better able to respect, cooperate with, and learn from colleagues whose classroom techniques are utterly different from mine. I am also able to alert my students to help me be on guard against some personal peculiarities. For example, I am such an extremely random learner that it takes stern discipline for me to organize material sequentially; I don't even read books from start to finish, but just open up the pages anywhere and begin reading. Almost always there is one student in the class who gazes at me with relief and wonder: "You do that too?"

The Role of the Teacher in a Student-Centered Classroom

When I consider my teaching practices now, they all seem interconnected: one belief implies a cluster of others. I believe that if learners are to be successful, the teacher needs to respect different routes to learning. The teacher who models this respect by encouraging students to follow their own interests, work at their own level, and try a variety of approaches finds that these students will take more responsibility for directing and assessing their own learning. Classroom assessment also necessarily becomes more responsive to learning *processes* as well as *outcomes*, giving a better rounded picture of the learner's capabilities. It's too early to tell yet, but the portfolio system now being tried in Vermont seems a promising step away from the authoritarian batteries of standardized tests that are now, regrettably, the national norm for assessment.

I believe that teachers who step away from the center of their classroom, in deference to the individual needs and interests of their students, also yield the prerogative to say exactly what's to be studied there and what's to be considered true. This is especially difficult for high school teachers, who have a good deal of academic content to put across. But they have as well a classroom full of allies. Instead of being central authority figures, teachers become role models, managers, and expert resources. As teachers respect the differences and seek the strengths among their students, those students come by degrees to accept each other's differences and to learn from each other. Teachers and students together begin to find their commonalities and to build a classroom culture based on mutual cooperation and respect. And as we have seen, a wonderful technique for bringing about this sense of community, particularly in an English class, is to share stories.

Problems in Teaching Mechanics

A teacher who emphasizes individual learning and the reading, writing, and sharing of stories will naturally deemphasize group lessons in spelling, grammar, and punctuation. For a book about teaching English, this one has very little to say about the *mechanics* of writing. It is not because I believe these skills to be unimportant; on the contrary, they are vital to effective writing. I *do* believe that more precious hours of schooling are wasted in trying to teach these subdisciplines than in any other way. The problem arises because of confusion about the nature of what's being taught. The rules of usage are not a body of knowledge; they have no value in and of themselves. They are a set of tools whose purpose is to facilitate communication.

When students have something to say, something they want to communicate, they can learn more grammar in five minutes than in a month of worksheets. Students who are offered a rule in a cognitive vacuum find it neither interesting nor memorable. When they *need* a rule to say something important, they learn it quickly and securely. To teach English grammar out of the context of writing is like teaching driver ed without a car, yet many people try to do it. My favorite definition of teachers who put rules before communication appears in *Zen and the Art of Motorcycle Maintenance*:

> This was the old slap-on-the-fingers-if-your-modifiers-were-caught-dangling stuff. *Correct* spelling, *correct* punctuation, *correct* grammar. Hundreds of itsy-bitsy rules for itsy-bitsy people. No one could remember all that stuff and concentrate on what he was trying to write about. (Pirsig 1974, 177, emphasis in original)

Phaedrus, the character through whom Pirsig is speaking, tries to exemplify and evoke what he terms *Quality* in his college freshman writing classes. He runs into problems because education is supposed to be rule-based, rational, and assessable, but he sees *Quality* as the realization in writing of each individual's unique vision. Is *Quality* absolute, capable of being defined by structural rules of discourse, the same for everyone? Or does it lie in the honesty and human truth of the individual utterance? This is the same conflict faced by a teacher who emphasizes narrative learning. Obviously I concur with Pirsig's preference, but in my classes I try, at least, to have it both ways. It is crucial for the teacher to have a sense of when to encourage the adolescent's emergent self and when to supply the rules that fit that self into the cultural norms.

Most, not all, of the student writings that appear in this book are final drafts. By the time they are ready for a grade, my students' papers are pretty accurate. This is true for a number of reasons. First, the students are interested in and proud of their papers and are therefore willing to put in the time and effort necessary to make them correct. They have had the opportunity to choose their own topic, and often they have been able to pick one from several discovery drafts to rework and submit. They have discussed one or more early drafts in conference and edited a late draft of their writing with the help of classmates. Throughout the process, they have had access to the powerful writing and editing tools of a word processor.

The Power of the Computer in the Writing Class

I believe in cooperative learning, and I believe in tools. I won't accept a paper until it has been submitted for conference and edited by peers, neatly typed, and run through the computer's spell-check feature. Some older students use a grammar checking program as well. Anything teenagers can use to help them learn and communicate their learning is all to the good. There is a large and growing body of literature that attests to the efficacy of computers in promoting growth in quantity and quality of student writing (Owston, Murphy, and Wideman 1992).

Students who are actively engaged in a writing workshop, dealing with their own work and that of their peers, are learning grammar, spelling, and mechanics as an integral part of the writing process. When the need arises, I teach these skills one-on-one, usually hovering over a still infinitely mutable document on the computer screen. If some mechanical problem is interfering with the student's effort to communicate effectively, I say, "Look, I'm going to teach you something useful." The lesson that follows takes only two or three minutes. It is immediately visible on the screen in a context of vital interest to the student. And the emphasis remains on *good writing*.

Some schools do not have adequate computer facilities. I believe that this is a short-sighted economy in today's society, but a writing workshop doesn't really need computer access. Although it's more tedious to draft and redraft by hand, I taught successful workshops before our computer lab was established. Even now, some students who are happy to use computer technology to produce a legible, correct final draft still don't like to compose at the keyboard. By the time writers have reached adolescence, it's none of the teacher's business how they choose to compose in the early drafts; whatever works is fine. I used to tell my classes that they could write the rough draft in lipstick on toilet paper if they so chose—until one ninth-grade boy did it. Goodness knows where he mustered all that lipstick.

Practical Matters

Both cooperative learning and computer-assisted learning occur during the keyboard conference. Students sit two to a terminal. Each in turn brings up onto the screen a paper in progress, and together they do a close, critical reading of both papers, revising and correcting as they go. I circulate, helping writers and readers resolve questions or disagreements about grammar, organization, mechanics, and usage.

Conclusion: The Teacher as Oracle

Strange, sometimes wonderful things happen when adolescents are encouraged to make choices about what they learn, or how and why they go about learning it. An English teacher seldom has real need to stand up in front of the class and act as an authority on certain subject matter. The authority exists, but it is shared; students and teachers become partners in learning. When I started my first teaching job many years ago, the department chairman told me never to forget: "The teacher is god in the classroom." I've puzzled often over that arrogant advice. In the end, I've decided that a really good and lucky teacher may instead be perceived as one through whom the gods speak: an oracle.

An oracle does not tell the truth. An oracle makes enigmatic pronouncements that guide the seeker to recognize a truth he already possesses. Every teacher may be an oracle, but none more so than the English teacher, whose job is not so much to transmit a body of knowledge as to help students develop the linguistic tools that access knowledge. Our subject area is made up of the stuff of human experience, the individual stories that define our society's truths. English teachers are as much engaged in issues of morality, self-recognition, and cultural identity as in academic content. It is our responsibility to guide each student to discover the truths of his culture, to build upon them, and to communicate the truths within himself.

Students are not all active seekers of truth. Maybe, instead of "The Teacher as Oracle," it's more realistic to think of "The Teacher as Cheerleader," because so much of our time and energy is spent trying to rouse some enthusiasm from the back row (one good reason for abolishing rows in the classroom). The cheerleader image is not apt, though, because it calls up associations of competition, winners and losers. The minute a teacher perceives any student as a loser, that kid's lost. The teacher needs *not* to be god in the classroom, but to be as human as possible. She needs to remember that behind the "obscenities and silence" are young egos, vulnerable and strong, afraid of failure but eager to grow. Every one of them is capable of learning, and each has a treasure trove of stories to tell.

Further Reading

This listing contains important sources that influenced my thinking and writing.

Armstrong, Michael. 1980. *Closely Observed Children: The Diary of a Primary Classroom*. London: Writers and Readers, Chameleon.

Atwell, Nancie. 1987. *In the Middle: Writing, Reading, and Learning with Adolescents*. Portsmouth, NH: Boynton/Cook.

Britton, James. 1970. *Language and Learning*. London: Penguin Books.

Elbow, Peter. 1981. *Writing with Power*. New York, Oxford: Oxford University Press.

Graves, Donald H. 1983. *Writing: Teachers & Children at Work*. Portsmouth, NH: Heinemann.

Halliday, M.A.K. 1975. "Learning How to Mean: Explorations in the Development of Language." In *Explorations in Language Study*, edited by Peter Doughty and Geoffrey Thornton. London: Edward Arnold.

Herndon, James. 1971. *How to Survive in Your Native Land*. New York: Simon and Schuster.

Holt, John. 1964. *How Children Fail*. New York: Dell Publishing Co.

Martin, Wallace. 1986. *Recent Theories of Narrative*. Ithaca and London: Cornell University Press.

Miller, Jane, editor. 1984. *Eccentric Propositions: Essays on Literature and the Curriculum*. London: Routledge and Kegan Paul.

Moffett, James. 1981. *Active Voice: A Writing Program Across the Curriculum*. Portsmouth, NH: Boynton/Cook.

Williams, Raymond. 1983. *Writing in Society*. London: Verso.

Works Cited

Bakhtin, M.M. 1986. "The Problem of Speech Genres." In *Speech Genres and Other Late Essays*, edited by Caryl Emerson and Michael Holquist. Austin: University of Texas Press.

Benjamin, Walter. 1969. *Illuminations: Essays and Reflections*. New York: Schocken Books.

Berthoff, Warner. 1970. "Fiction, History, Myth: Notes Toward the Discrimination of Narrative Forms." In *The Interpretation of Narrative Theory and Practice*, edited by Morton W. Bloomfield. Cambridge, MA: Harvard University Press.

Bettelheim, Bruno. 1977. *The Uses of Enchantment: The Meaning and Importance of Fairy Tales*. New York: Random House, Vintage Books.

Brandt, Deborah. 1992. "The Cognitive as the Social: An Ethnomethodological Approach to Writing Process Research." *Written Communication* 9(3), 315–55.

Brannon, Lil. 1985. "Toward a Theory of Composition." In *Perspectives on Research and Scholarship in Composition*, edited by Ben W. McClelland and Timothy R. Donovan. New York: MLA.

Brewer, Lawrence. 1992. Conversation. Bristol, VT. May 20.

Britton, James. 1970. *Language and Learning*. London: Penguin Books.

————. 1982. *Prospect and Retrospect: Selected Essays of James Britton*, edited by Gordon M. Pradl. Portsmouth, NH: Boynton/Cook.

Britton, James, Tony Burgess, Nancy Martin, Alex McLeod, and Harold Rosen. 1975. *The Development of Writing Abilities (11–18)*. Houndmills Basingstoke Hampshire: MacMillan Education.

Brooke, Robert E. 1991. *Writing and Sense of Self*. Urbana, IL: NCTE.

Bruner, Jerome. 1986. *Actual Minds, Possible Worlds*. Cambridge, MA: Harvard University Press.

———. 1990. *Acts of Meaning*. Cambridge, MA: Harvard University Press.

Burgess, Tony. 1988. "Cultural and Linguistic Diversity and English Teaching." In *The Word for Teaching Is Learning: Essays for James Britton*, edited by Martin Lightfoot and Nancy Martin. London: Heinemann.

———. 1990. Conversation with author. Oxford, July 11.

Campbell, Joseph, with Bill Moyers. 1988. *The Power of Myth*. New York: Doubleday, Anchor Books.

Cazden, Courtney. 1988. "Social Interaction as Scaffold: The Power and Limits of a Metaphor." In *The Word for Teaching Is Learning: Essays for James Britton*, edited by Martin Lightfoot and Nancy Martin. London: Heinemann.

Clausen, Christopher. 1991. "'Canon,' Theme, and Code." In *The Hospitable Canon: Essays on Literary Play, Scholarly Choice, and Popular Pressures. Cultura Ludens* Vol. 4, edited by Virgil Nemoianu and Robert Royal. Amsterdam and Philadelphia: John Benjamins Publishing Company.

Cole, Michael, and Sylvia Scribner. 1978. "Introduction." In *Mind In Society* by L.S. Vygotsky, edited by Michael Cole, Vera John-Steiner, Sylvia Scribner, and Ellen Souberman. Cambridge, MA: Harvard University Press.

Coles, Robert. 1989. *The Call of Stories: Teaching and the Moral Imagination*. Boston: Houghton Mifflin.

Cooper, Joanne E. 1991. "Telling Our Own Stories: The Reading and Writing of Journals or Diaries." In *Stories Lives Tell: Narrative and Dialogue in Education*, edited by Carol Witherell and Nel Noddings. New York: Teachers College Press.

Cooper, Kenneth J. 1990. "Head Start Endures, Making a Difference." *The Washington Post*, April 22, A12.

Culler, Jonathan. 1976. *Saussure*. Fontana Modern Masters, edited by Frank Kermode. London: Fontana Press.

de Castell, Suzanne, and Allan Luke. 1989. "Literacy Instruction: Technology and Technique." In *Language Authority and*

Criticism: Readings on the School Textbook, edited by Suzanne de Castell, Allan Luke, and Carmen Luke. London: The Falmer Press.

Dixon, John, and Leslie Stratta. 1986. *Writing Narrative – And Beyond*. Canada: The Canada Council of Teachers of English.

Egan, Kieran. 1989. "The Shape of the Science Text." In *Language, Authority and Criticism*, edited by Suzanne de Castell, Allan Luke, and Carmen Luke. London: The Falmer Press.

Elbow, Peter. 1973. *Writing Without Teachers*. London, Oxford, and New York: Oxford University Press.

Feldman, Carol Fleisher. 1989. "Monologue as Problem-Solving Narrative." In *Narratives from the Crib*, edited by Katherine Nelson. Cambridge, MA: Harvard University Press.

Fox, Carol. 1989. "Divine Dialogues: The Role of Argument in the Narrative Discourse of a Five-Year-Old Storyteller." In *Narrative & Argument*, edited by Richard Andrews. Philadelphia: Open University Press.

Francis, Dick. 1990. *Longshot*. New York: G.P. Putnam's Sons.

Halliday, M.A.K. 1989. *Spoken and Written Language*. Oxford: Oxford University Press.

Hardy, Barbara. 1977. "Narrative as a Primary Act of Mind." In *The Cool Web*, edited by Margaret Meek, Aidan Warlow, and Griselda Barton. London: Bodley Head.

Henry, Tamara. 1992. "Survey: Workers Need Better Communication Skills." *The Burlington Free Press*, Sept. 22.

Hesse, Douglas. 1989. "Persuading as Storying: Essays, Narrative Rhetoric, and the College Writing Course." In *Narrative and Argument*, edited by Richard Andrews. Philadelphia: Milton Keynes, Open University Press.

Hobsbawm, E. J. 1987. *The Age of Empire 1875–1914*. London: Weidenfeld and Nicolson.

Huddle, David. 1991. "Taking What You Need, Giving What You Can: The Writer as Student and Teacher." In *Writers on Writing*, edited by Robert Pack and Jay Parini. Hanover and London: University Press of New England, Middlebury College Press.

Keirsey, David, and Marilyn Bates. 1984. *Please Understand Me: Character & Temperament Types*. Del Mar, CA: Prometheus Nemesis Book Company.

Kingston, Maxine Hong. 1977. *The Woman Warrior*. New York: Random House, Vintage Books.

Labov, W. 1972. "The Logic of Nonstandard English." In *Language and Social Context*, edited by Pier Paolo Giglioli. London: Penguin Books.

Lane, Barry. 1992. Interview with author. Charlotte, Vermont, February 12.

———. 1993. *Writing as a Road to Self-Discovery*. Cincinnati, OH: Writer's Digest Books.

Lawrence, Gale. 1990. Writers Workshop. Ferrisburgh, VT, June 14.

Levy, Elena. 1989. "Monologue as Development of the Text-Forming Function of Language." In *Narrative from the Crib*, edited by Katherine Nelson. Cambridge, MA: Harvard University Press.

Macrorie, Ken. 1984. *Writing to be Read*. Portsmouth, NH: Boynton/Cook.

Mair, Miller. 1976. "Metaphors for Living." *Nebraska Symposium on Motivation*, 1976.

Martin, Nancy. 1983. *Mostly About Writing: Selected Essays*. Portsmouth, NH: Boynton/Cook.

Mathieson, Margaret. 1987. "The Newbolt Report and English for the English." In *English Literature in Schools*, edited by V.J. Lee. Philadelphia: Milton Keynes, Open University Press.

Moss, Gemma. 1989. *Un/Popular Fictions*. London: Virago.

Murray, Donald. 1984. *Write to Learn*. New York: Holt, Rinehart and Winston.

Nelson, Katherine, editor. 1989. *Narratives from the Crib*. Cambridge, MA: Harvard University Press.

Ong, Walter J. 1982. *Orality and Literacy: The Technologizing of the Word*. London and New York: Routledge.

Owston, Ronald D., Sharon Murphy, and Herbert H. Wideman. 1992. "The Effects of Word Processing on Students' Writing

Quality and Revision Strategies." *Research in the Teaching of English* 26(3): 249–76.

Pace, Barbara G. 1992. "The Textbook Canon: Genre, Gender and Race in US Literature Anthologies." *English Journal*, Sept., 33–38.

Pagano, Jo Anne. 1991. "Moral Fictions: The Dilemma of Theory and Practice." In *Stories Lives Tell: Narrative and Dialogue in Education*, edited by Carol Witherell and Nel Noddings. New York: Teachers College Press.

Pirsig, Robert M. 1974. *Zen and the Art of Motorcycle Maintenance*. Toronto, New York, London: Bantam Books.

Polkinghorne, Donald E. 1988. *Narrative Knowing and the Human Sciences*. Albany: State University of New York Press.

Polster, Erving. 1987. *Every Person's Life Is Worth a Novel*. New York and London: W.W. Norton & Company.

Rosen, Betty. 1988. *And None of It Was Nonsense: The Power of Storytelling in School*. London: Mary Glasgow Publications.

Shakespeare, William. 1958. *A Midsummer Night's Dream*. New York: Simon & Schuster, Pocket Books.

Silko, Leslie Marmon. 1981. *Storyteller*. New York: Arcade Publishing.

Simons, Elizabeth Radin. 1990. *Student Worlds, Student Words: Teaching Writing Through Folklore*. Portsmouth, NH: Boynton/Cook.

Steinem, Gloria. 1992. *Revolution from Within: A Book of Self-Esteem*. Boston: Little, Brown and Company.

Thompson, William Irwin. 1989. *Imaginary Landscapes: Making Worlds of Myth and Science*. New York: St. Martin's Press.

Trimbur, John. 1985. "Collaborative Learning and Teaching Writing." In *Perspectives on Research and Scholarship in Composition*, edited by Ben W. McClelland and Timothy R. Donovan. New York: MLA.

Twain, Mark. 1918. *Huckleberry Finn*. Reprint. New York: Pocket Books. 1958.

Vygotsky, Lev. 1978. *Mind in Society: The Development of Higher Psychological Processes*, edited by Michael Cole, Vera John-Steiner, Sylvia Scribner, and Ellen Souberman. Cambridge, MA: Harvard University Press.

———. 1986. *Thought and Language.* Edited by Alex Kozulin. Cambridge, MA: MIT Press.

Wald, Alan. 1989. "Hegemony and Literary Tradition in the United States." In *Language Authority and Criticism: Readings on the School Textbook*, edited by Suzanne de Castell, Allan Luke, and Carmen Luke. London: The Falmer Press.

Wertsch, James V. 1991. *Voices of the Mind: A Sociocultural Approach to Mediated Action.* Cambridge, MA: Harvard University Press.

Worthen, Julie. 1992. "Kids and Families Get a Leg Up with Head Start's Help." *Chicago Tribune*, Jan. 12, 18:8.

Young, Art. 1986. "Rebuilding Community in the English Department." In *Writing Across the Disciplines: Research Into Practice*, edited by Art Young and Toby Fulwiler. Portsmouth, NH: Boynton/Cook.

Zachmann, William F. 1991. "Education: The Final Frontier." *PC Magazine*, Aug., 97.

Zinsser, William. 1987. "Writing and Remembering: A Memoir and an Introduction." In *Inventing the Truth: The Art and Craft of Memoir*, edited by William Zinsser. Boston: Houghton Mifflin Company.

Index

Adolescent writers, 8, 122, 135, 146; of autobiography; 101, 103–106, 145; of dialogue, 36; of genre, 67; of journals, 125, 126; of metaphor, 116–118; as mythmakers, 30, 31; of transactional prose, 136, 139, 142, 149, 153

Adolescents, 55, 64, 76, 101; conceptual development of, 6, 7, 79, 135; and creativity, 90; and daydreams, 29, 133; and fabulous literature, 27, 29–31; and learning, 10, 11, 21, 22, 30, 131, 136, 149, 160; and narrative, 8, 10, 11, 21, 22, 58; and popular fiction, 65, 66, 72; and public speaking, 41, 46; as readers, 51, 94; teachers of, 4, 7, 12, 19, 131, 140, 155; and values, 34, 104

Adventure fantasy, 28, 32, 67

American literature, 44, 78, 85

Analysis, 21; character, 138, 146, 154; and experience, 11; literary, 7, 21, 81, 138, 149; and narrative, 123, 132, 139, 154; as a rhetorical form, 5, 8, 11, 40, 80, 89, 131, 137, 143; in student writing, 81, 109, 137, 138, 142

Anthologies, 85, 86

Argument: in academic discourse, 20; in the curriculum, 19; in expressive writing, 131–33; and learning, 11; in literary criticism, 90; and narrative, 116, 139, 140, 154; as a rhetorical form, 5, 123, 131, 143; in student writing, 4, 137

Art: and culture, 64, 84, 90; interpretation of, 89; literature as, 68, 83; narrative as, 19, 40, 50; and narrative truth, 15, 28; in school, 94; in student writing, 8, 31, 33, 34, 36, 53, 107, 127, 128

Assessment, 7, 8, 89, 136, 150, 157

Audience: peers as, 145; student fear of, 42; teacher as, 7

Author: as authority, 103; and culture, 51, 79, 83, 86; as individual, 83; stance of, 115; as storyteller, 14, 79; student as, 23, 31, 32, 67, 74, 92, 100, 114, 144–46, 154; and voice, 106

Authority: adult, 101, 122; of autobiographical narrator, 101; in the classroom, 161; cultural, 41; in a democracy, 33;

41; and language, 127; moral, 31, 33, 41; of oral storyteller, 45; of public speaker, 42; teacher as, 26, 157, 161

Authors: canonic, 85, 86, 89; from oral cultures, 44, 45; and student readers, 50–52, 79, 80, 89, 90, 92

Autobiographical writing: adolescent, 103 (*see also* Adolescent writers); benefits of, 101; in the classroom, 102; definition of, 103; in the literature class, 108; as a transitional genre, 145; voice in, 106

Autobiography: as narrative, 103; *The Woman Warrior,* 61

Bakhtin, M.M., 11, 20, 91

Ballads, 58, 59

Bard, 38, 91

Bates, Marilyn, 156

Benjamin, Walter, 40, 41

Berthoff, Warner, 30, 32

Bettelheim, Bruno, 29, 32

Biographical essay, 153, 154

Blue books, 128

Brandt, Deborah, 21

Brannon, Lil, 7, 31

Brewer, Lawrence, 151, 152

Britton, James, 4, 8, 20, 111, 114, 122, 124, 132

Brooke, Robert E., 100, 143, 144

Bruner, Jerome, 15, 16, 18, 21, 83, 111

Burgess, Tony, 6, 8, 65

Campbell, Joseph, 21, 28, 33

Canon, the, 76; in American Literature, 78; and creativity, 79, 88; cultural bias of, 46, 70, 78, 84–86; definition of, 64, 84–86; English curriculum and, 64, 78, 85; as knowledge, 63; as open text, 88; teaching, 85, 86, 89, 94; under attack, 85; vs. popular genres, 65, 87, 88

Cazden, Courtney, 57

Character analysis, 138, 146, 154

Character sketch, 143, 146, 147

Chomsky, Noam, 20

Classroom, the: community, 102, 105; conversation in, 9, 41; cultural diversity in, 8, 32, 43, 61, 65, 72; culture, 4, 43, 51,

143; as genre, 142; of literary criticism, 80, 131; models of, 143; of personal narrative, 116; "The Storyteller," 40; and the student writer, 139, 140, 142, 143, 147; transition to, from narrative, 149; "Writing to Learn and Learning to Write," 114
Evaluation, 91, 102, 107, 109, 115, 116
Experience: cultural, 62, 79, 161; as data, 40, 41; drama as, 17; and expressive language, 123, 132, 137; and learning, 7, 11, 13, 22, 50, 55, 65, 105, 111, 149; literature as, 4, 161; myth as, 40; narrative as, 14, 16, 17, 22, 99, 103; reading as, 16, 79, 80, 89; sensory, 46, 112; as shaped by narrative, 10, 11, 15, 17, 19, 100, 103, 114, 117; shared, through narrative, 4, 8, 12, 14, 40, 43, 55, 58, 95, 102, 105; through reenactment, 50–52, 54, 55, 57, 58; and truth, 14, 15, 19
Exposition: in expressive language, 123, 131, 132; and the learner, 11; and narrative, 11; as rhetorical form, 5, 8, 11, 40, 143; in student writing, 143, 145, 147
Expressive language, 122–28, 132, 136

Fable, 26, 28, 33, 34, 36, 45
Fabulous genres, 28
Fantasy, 5, 26–28, 32, 66, 67, 75, 103
Feldman, Carol Fleisher, 132
Feminism, 85
Fiction: American, 78; canon of, the, 78; creativity in, 83; fabulous, 30–32; popular, 65, 67, 69, 70, 72; science, 28; and the storyteller, 15; in student writing, 8, 29, 32, 66, 72, 103; and truth, 15, 18, 99, 103
First person, 103, 104, 150
Folk tales, 26, 31, 32
Folklore, 21, 28, 43, 51
Form: essay as, 142; and genre, 68, 133, 134, 137; linguistic, 7, 17, 29, 59, 132; literary, 65, 72, 103; narrative, 10, 17, 18, 28, 31, 34, 66, 94, 118, 152; in popular fiction, 66–68, 72; as rules of culture, 68, 127; in student writing, 7, 8, 66–68, 70, 72, 115, 118, 135, 136, 145, 151, 152
Forms of behavior, developmental, 5, 113; of discourse, 7, 131; of reenactment, 58, 89; rhetorical, 5, 8; rhetorical, teaching of, 9, 10, 19, 131, 144; transactional, 10, 131, 135, 136, 144; transitional, 144, 146
Formula fiction, 65
Fox, Carol, 34, 140
Francis, Dick, 29

Generalization, 80; and adolescent development, 135, 142
Genre: the canon as, 70; classroom language as, 51; concept of, 23, 65; cultural, 22, 65, 67, 68, 70, 72; and culture, 66; the essay as, 142; and expressive language, 122, 126, 133; hybrid, in student writing, 7, 8, 150, 151, 153; rules of, 65; scholarly writing as, 131; and the student writer, 65, 77, 134, 136, 140, 148; and teaching, 72
Genres: fabulous, 28; hybrid, 7, 142, 150, 153; of literature, 67, 134; "magic," 29; nonfiction, 143; relationships among, 139; speech, 52; transitional, 143
Genres, literary: ballad, 58; descriptive essay, 118; folk tale, 29; myth, 29; short story, 76
Genres, local: "The Hunt," 68; "Narrative of Place," 118
Genres, popular, 22, 23, 65, 66; and curriculum, 87; "Dungeons and Dragons," 67; fantasy in, 67; rules of, 66, 72; and the student reader, 67, 76; and the student writer, 66, 68, 72–74, 94; and teaching, 69; vs. the canon, 87, 88
Genres, transitional: the character sketch, 146; the definition essay, 143, 147; personal narrative essay, 143, 145; the process paper, 143, 145
Good writing, 52, 102, 134, 139, 140, 144, 148, 160
Gossip 8, 18, 41, 122
Grammar, 6, 19, 158–60
Guided imagery, 118

Halliday, M.A.K., 20, 42
Hardy, Barbara, 18
Head Start, 71
Henry, Tamara, 135
Hesse, Douglas, 112
Hobsbawm, E.J., 117
Homer, 38, 43, 90, 91, 93
Huckleberry Finn, 9, 21, 55
Huddle, David, 104, 143
"Hunt, The," 68, 76

Image, 10, 35, 36, 80, 82, 86, 104, 111, 161
Imagination, 83; and creativity, 14; and metaphor, 5; in mythmaking, 27, 28; in the reader, 16, 50; in student narrative, 10, 26, 82; and truth, 103
Inner speech, 127
Integrative thinking, 151
Invention, 54, 80